A NEW WAY OF LIVING

Practicing the Beatitudes Every Day

OTHER NEW HOPE BOOKS BY GENE WILKES

Character: The Pulse of a Disciple's Heart

Coauthored with Norman Blackaby

GENE
WILKES

A NEW WAY OF LIVING

Practicing the Beatitudes Every Day

NEW HOPE
PUBLISHERS
Gospel-Centered. Missions-Driven.
BIRMINGHAM, ALABAMA

New Hope® Publishers
P. O. Box 12065
Birmingham, AL 35202-2065
NewHopeDigital.com
New Hope Publishers is a division of WMU®.

Library of Congress Cataloging-in-Publication Data
Wilkes, C. Gene.
A new way of living : practicing the beatitudes every day / Gene Wilkes.
p. cm.
Includes bibliographical references and index.
ISBN 978-1-59669-365-4 (pbk.)
1. Beatitudes--Criticism, interpretation, etc. I. Title.
BT382.W54 2013
241.5'3--dc23
2012034901

Cover Design: Michel Lê
Interior Design: Glynese Northam

ISBN-10: 1-59669-365-7
ISBN-13: 978-1-59669-365-4
N134108 • 0113 • 3M1

Acknowledgments

All of the exercises I do, I do best with a partner or in groups. My spiritual life is done best that way, and so is my writing. I am never as good a communicator alone as I am in a team. I want to thank Andrea Mullins, Joyce Dinkins, and Tina Atchenson on the New Hope team who made this project possible and who put it in its best form for you, the reader. I also could not have written this book without the writing partnership of Cheryll Duffie, who also happens to be the mother of my youngest daughter's husband! Cheryll's humorous and popular style has made my sometime heady thoughts appealing to many more readers. I am indebted to her for her many original thoughts and patient rewrites of the manuscript. I also want to thank my Leader and the One on whom I keep my eyes, Jesus. His example of endurance and victory on the Cross is the greatest act of love and compassion known in human history. No one has matched His physical, emotional, and spiritual victory to defeat evil and death, our two greatest enemies. His creation, in which we run, ride, and hike is a gift to us all and a gift we too often overlook as we live and dwell in our handmade worlds. May we tread lightly as we run with all our hearts.

Dedication

To my brothers and sisters in Christ who run, ride, and hike with me and who seek to follow Jesus' ways and words of life.

Table of Contents

INTRODUCTION

Who wouldn't be up for "a new way of living"?[1] How often is it that all the major areas of your life are hitting on all cylinders? Just when you think things are going good on the home front, the boss throws a major project your way that's going to demand all that you've been giving . . . and more. Or, maybe you're really serious about developing and sticking with some semblance of an exercise regimen and your knee goes out. Or, maybe . . . the point is: the times when everything is going great in every area of life are few and far between *and* short-lived when they are even present! I say that not to discourage or frustrate you, but to encourage you that "a new way of living" can be as simple as taking the stairs instead of the elevator, or reading just three verses a day from the Bible, or extending a compliment to an equally overextended co-worker. Stay with me, friend. I can sense the skepticism and we're only a paragraph into this journey.

I promise a new way of living really is *that* simple.

In all my years of preaching, teaching, running, cycling, growing, and learning, I've come to a startling discovery about wellness and its pursuit: *It is achieved one choice at a time.* That's it. Incredibly simple, isn't it? This new way of living that's yours for the doing all comes down to one single, solitary decision at a time. Reminds me of the ancient adage that goes, "A journey of

> Exercise doesn't create the gift; it enhances it.

a thousand miles begins with a single step."

The same holds true for all areas of wellness, whether it is emotional, spiritual, mental, or physical. It is a matter of being proactive in our pursuit and being preventative in the measures we take to head off likely challenges and temptations. It's a delicate balancing act—what with planning ahead to make sure there are carrots in your desk drawer to snack on instead of Hershey's Kisses and making actual write-it-in-ink appointments with yourself to exercise physically *and* rest, refuel, and reenergize your emotional self, all the while trying to honor your resolution to grow spiritually. Add 2.3 kids (OK, maybe just 2 *whole* kids), a laundry pile you haven't seen the bottom of in weeks, and a lawn that announces to the neighborhood your obvious neglect, and suddenly you're juggling more commitments and demands on your time than a circus clown has spinning hoops. I said pursuing wellness in our lives is simple . . . but that doesn't mean it's *easy.*

I know all too well how the most insignificant conflicts to your schedule can turn into time-zapping, priority-busting, there's-always-tomorrow inroads into your best-laid plans. I know because, despite the fact I encourage, teach, and lead people for a living, this morning I cheated on my morning workout. Big deal, you say. Make it up tomorrow, Wilkes. What's the worst thing that can happen if some runnin' dude doesn't get his shot of endorphins today? Let me explain.

I was training for a marathon when I wrote this, and the schedule called for eight miles tempo. I ran only seven and never really sustained my race-day pace. Of course, I had good excuses. *The workout's hard, and my aging joints are sore. The weather's bad, and I've already completed the other runs scheduled for the week. Surely my earlier runs will compensate for this shortened one.*

Good excuses. Bad results. If I don't stick to my preparation schedule, I'll never run the race I hope to run—no matter the quality of my excuses.

Believe it or not, my incomplete workout today will affect my performance even though the event is ten weeks away. Endurance is built by placing one workout upon the other. You must be consistent over the long haul to run successfully.

What I did that morning is what too many of us do every day in our spiritual training. We have great excuses for cutting our time short with God. We then wonder why we find ourselves falling short of where we want to be in our relationship with Jesus. Hurried schedules, cluttered lives, and urgent tasks push our endurance-building time to the end of the day, week, or month. Soon we can only remember when we were spiritually fit as we succumb to the battle of urgency over what is important.

I like to think of it this way: Exercise doesn't create the gift; it enhances it. Spiritual exercises allow the gift God has placed in your life to grow and mature. You fast to replace addictions with adoration. You learn to be silent to hear the "still, small voice of God." You give freely to help break the bonds of personal materialism. Spiritual exercises such as these build the spiritual endurance you need to overcome temptation and finish the race of faith.

The Gospel of Luke tells the story of one man and his conflicted desire to follow Jesus. In it, the man said to Jesus, "I will follow you, Lord; but first let me go back and say good-bye to my family." Jesus replied, "No one who puts his hand to the plow and looks back is fit for service in the kingdom of God" (Luke 9:61–62). For Jesus, saying good-bye to family wasn't a good excuse. His command was then as it is now: once you commit to follow Him, never look back. Can the excuses. You don't offer to follow Jesus on your terms any more than you commit to running a marathon but only complete *half* the training program. To follow Jesus on your terms is denial that Jesus is Lord of your life. Jesus insists that if you follow Him, you must actually do what He says to do, act the way He says to act, and rest when He says to rest.

The next time the workout says run eight miles tempo, you can bet I'll go the distance, regardless of my excuses, because I want to race well and because I realize that working toward a new way of living is a day-by-day, moment-by-moment opportunity to know and follow Christ.[2]

This book is a journey with Jesus that will create a new way of living for you. It is not really "new" in the sense of something that's never been done before because Jesus' words and ways are ancient, tried and proven. But this way of life is new in the sense of being fresh like a second chance or the sunrise after a sleepless night. Jesus' inaugural words form the basis of our path to experience life as God designed it, and our one-choice-at-a-time progress will guide us into a deeper relationship with God and others.

We will be as honest with you as we can with our own struggles, and we will portray the words of Jesus as authentically as we know how. We are not perfect specimens of physical or spiritual health, but we hope sharing our struggles with you will help us all find the new way of living as we follow Jesus more closely together.

CHAPTER 1

Spiritual Health in Total Wellness

For physical training is of some value, but godliness has value for all things, holding promise for both the present life and the life to come.

—1 Timothy 4:8

I could not take a deep breath. Each time I tried to inhale deeply my chest would tighten, and I could not get the breath I needed. I looked at the clock. It was 2:00 A.M. on a Monday morning after a long Sunday of ministry. I lay in my bed for another two hours until I knew I had to do something. My parents had come to see their grandchildren in the Christmas musical and were staying the night with us. I slipped out of bed trying not to wake my wife, Kim, and asked my father for one of his nitro pills. They worked for him. "Why not me?" I reasoned. We whispered about whether or not that was a good idea, and I decided to put one under my tongue. I went back to bed with little change in how I felt. At 6:30 when Kim woke up, I told her how I was feeling, and we all agreed my father should take me to the hospital to see what was up.

Three days later after every heart test known at the time, or so it seemed, I left the hospital diagnosed with heart disease and doctor's orders that my stress-filled life had to change.

I was 40 years old, 20 pounds overweight, the father of a 7- and 10-year-old, a husband, pastor of a fast-growing church in transition, a writer, conference leader, and I was convinced all of it was necessary to live a full and meaningful life. In all of my activity to live out what I thought was God's call on my life, I had not cared for my body, and my soul was as dry as a west Texas summer. The doctor essentially told me, "You can continue what you are doing and maybe live another ten years, or, you can change how you live and live as long as you want." I knew something had to change. But what?

During that period away from the church I took time to be outdoors—my favorite cathedral to worship God. I also took time to walk my daughters to and from school. I read for inspiration, not for my next sermon or conference. Ironically, I was in the middle of reading Eugene Peterson's book, *The Contemplative Pastor*, when all this happened. I picked it up and read it from the beginning again. I savored it like a cedar-plank, baked salmon dinner at a fine restaurant as my ministry and conference schedule came to a halt. Peterson challenged me by asking, "If I'm not busy making my mark in the world or doing what everyone expects me to do, what do I do?" He answered with what I knew was the truth: I can be a pastor who prays, preaches, and listens.[1]

One day after I returned home from the hospital, I took a walk on a nearby hike-and-bike trail near our home. When I returned home, I made this journal entry:

> A cool, crisp autumn breeze blew among the trees stripped of their leaves. I stopped by a stream to listen to its healing melody. At one point, I felt a joy

> and presence of God I had not felt in many months. The joy of the Lord had returned. Prayer and walking became the rhythm of the hour.

I knew that "rhythm of the hour" was the rhythm of life, but how would I live that pace when I returned to the needs of people and leading a church in transition—not to mention the needs of my wife and family? A couple of days later I wrote, "I have heard and seen my calling again. I look forward to the future with a new way of living." A *new way of living* was the phrase of life for me as I reflected on what I had written in the moment. But I still asked where would I find the time for what I knew was a life-giving pace? The words of the doctor and the thirst of my soul, however, insisted I find room for a new way of living or I would literally die.

I did change my lifestyle physically and spiritually. It was not easy to slow down or say no to ministry needs and opportunity. But I did. I fell in love with trail running, and my wonderful wife, Kim, taught me to eat healthy and hid the sweet stuff from me. I learned the joy of sitting and listening to God's Word and Spirit—and as a premature baby develops following birth, I learned to find the "rhythm of the hour" more times than not while the church continued to transform into God's vision. The Beatitudes became Jesus' benchmark and the path for my relationship with Him. My soul now breathes along with my body, and while I slip in my eating and exercise—both physically and spiritually—I continue on the path of this new way of life that has restored me to the life Jesus promised.

That incident with my heart was in 1993. Today, my daughters are married, and we are grandparents. I am still at our church after 25 years of ministry, I am writing a resource which I believe is not only the heart of Jesus' message for His followers but the path to a new way of living that can restore the joy of the Lord to your life. Jesus' ancient words we call the Beatitudes are the pathway to spiritual wellness we all long for, the wellness which is God's design for our lives.

What Do the Beatitudes Have to Do with Spiritual Wellness?

For centuries, Christians have recognized something special in the Beatitudes, the opening words of Jesus' Sermon on the Mount recorded in Matthew's story of Jesus, chapters 5 through 7. Perhaps it is the seemingly contradictory blessings that say so very much in just a few short verses. Who among us is going to be the first to volunteer to become *poor in spirit*? (I can hear your thoughts now: "Me? Volunteer to be poor? I don't know about you, but being 'poor' at anything is just not how I roll!") Do you think there'll be a big demand to be known as *meek*? (Can't you imagine being introduced at a party like this: "You know, John, don't you? He's meek.") And *persecuted for righteousness*? (Just the word *persecuted* kind of makes you want to run the other way, doesn't it?)

However, with a little prayerful reading, a little commentary explaining the *true* meaning of Jesus' words in the Beatitudes, and a heart open to growing in Christlikeness, gradually we can understand and appreciate the incredible wisdom in some of the most powerful and challenging words of Jesus. When we are able to see past what

> Wellness is a dynamic state.

many of us consider shortcomings at first glance (think *poor, mournful, meek*), we are able to realize that the Beatitudes are an intentionally ordered, divinely crafted list of characteristics that describe the inner wellness of a person who follows Jesus "with all your heart and with all your soul and with all your mind and with all your strength" (Mark 12:30).

Defining Wellness — Spiritual and Otherwise

When you mention wellness, most people will immediately make the association to their own personal physical state. You won't be far into the conversation before they start telling you how well-off they used to be ("Man, you should have seen my abs in high school—could've bounced a dime off 'em!"). Or, what they *should* be doing to improve their wellness ("Come next Monday, I'm running five miles a day—you watch me!"). Our tendency is almost always to associate wellness with physical well-being. And while our physical wellness (or lack of) is the most easily identified, most easily measured, and often provides the clearest path to improvement, it is important to note that our physical nature is just one dimension of our whole being.

As followers of Christ, the Bible tells us that physical wellness is of great importance, but concern for the state of our *spiritual* wellness should be above all else. Second Timothy 4:8 tells us clearly that in the quest for wellness, all other human dimensions are secondary to pursuing Christlikeness: "For physical training is of some value, but godliness has value for all things, holding promise for both the present life and the life to come." In other words, another hundred crunches will take you a step closer to rock hard abs, but they will fall dismally short toward affecting your eternal residence. Let me be clear, however, that these inspired words of Scripture are not to be construed as a carte blanche excuse to forgo your regular trip to the gym in lieu of an evening with your Bible . . . oh, and a bag of barbecue potato chips to munch on while you're reading! Without a doubt, the Lord wants us to pursue excellence in both areas, but we are to track the health of our souls decidedly more fervently.

Common Aspects of Wellness

There are three primary characteristics regarding the quest for wellness—be it physical, spiritual, or otherwise. When working toward wellness, it is helpful to remember that *wellness* is a dynamic state; *wellness* is a journey, not a destination; and *wellness* is best defined relatively, and therefore more personal and meaningful to each of us.

Let's apply these criteria to both physical and spiritual wellness. First, the easy example:

PHYSICAL WELLNESS

Wellness is a dynamic state. Consider your body temperature, blood pressure, pulse, and respiratory rate: your vital signs. Add to those your body weight. (Sorry, that is part of the picture.) Are any of these measurements the same today as they were yesterday? Are they even the same from the morning to the afternoon, and into the evening? Ask any dieters and they'll tell you a resounding, "No way!" They know all too well that our weight can vary as much as five to seven pounds over the course of a day. Likewise, our bodies are constantly changing, day by day, moment by moment in regard to what we put in them, what we challenge them to do for us, and how we allow them to rest and recoup. Our physical wellness operates in a wholly dynamic state—from the amount we can bench press one day to the next to the complete cellular regeneration that continually takes place within us every seven years. Physically, wellness is, without a doubt, one dynamic process after another, involving change upon change in our heavenly designed bodies.

Wellness is a journey, not a destination. Most people who are seriously committed to working toward physical wellness realize they will never fully arrive at a perfect physical state. Sure they'll set short-, mid-, and long-term goals to work toward, but deep down they realize that even if they accomplish the most challenging "stretch goal," there will still always be room for improvement. Maybe they could shave a few more strokes off their golf game, maybe they could beat their best cycling time by a few more seconds, or maybe they could finally master (and hold!) the advanced yoga position that has eluded them for years. Whatever your sport, exercise routine, or physical regimen, you'll save yourself much anguish and frustration once you accept that improvement, regardless of how slight, is the payoff. Being better today than you were yesterday or last week or last month is the goal.

Wellness is best defined relatively, and therefore is more personal and meaningful to each of us individually. Ever watch the old guy at the gym grab the overhead shoulder press machine as soon as you wipe it down and pull the pin from the stack of weights? "Sure, Pops, go ahead and take it down a notch or two," you think to yourself. Wait a minute—what's this? The old geezer is *adding* weights to your stack. Who does he think he is—Mr. Senior America? The old dude has more wrinkles than a Shar-Pei puppy and yet he's left you behind to eat his proverbial senior citizen dust! What is up with that?

Whether you're deflated and discouraged or motivated and inspired by others' physical wellness, we serve our selves best when we remind ourselves that, at day's end, we are our only measure of progress or decline against the measures of fitness we compare ourselves. Sure, there are generally accepted norms and ranges to aspire to in order to achieve or operate within, but we benefit ourselves the most when our basis of comparison is something as simple as a "before" picture, a baseline EKG, or a progressive chart showing our increased distances for our 45-minute run. Goals of all sorts are most intensely pursued and most genuinely relished when they are personal in nature. That can be both positive and negative, but in order to improve our physical prowess, our personal best should always be the benchmark.

SPIRITUAL WELLNESS

When you join a gym, the trainers usually give you some sort of physical assessment to determine muscle tone, body mass, agility, and endurance. Trainers then use these findings to help you identify fitness goals and establish a plan to accomplish them. They give you a baseline of measurements that help you realize where you stand in relation to your ideal condition and a road map on how to progress from there. Such is traditionally not the case for those seeking a similar game plan for spiritual wellness.

Few systematic spiritual assessments exist and, among those which do, few promote themselves as "comprehensive" or "exhaustive." It is imperative that we understand that even these are the reflection of individual interpretation based upon *their* education, *their* personal experiences, and *their* biblical worldview. The luxury of hard and fast clinical and measurable results such as EKG read-outs simply does not exist for spiritual wellness as they relate to determining spiritual wellness. We do, however, have the clear Word of God that spells out the measures by which God evaluates our character and tests our trust in Him so we can be His salt and light servants to others in the name of Jesus.

Let's return to the three tenets against which we characterized physical wellness and, this time, apply the principles to fitness on a spiritual level.

Wellness is a dynamic state. Just as physical wellness never remains static and is constantly subjected to a barrage of outside and internal influences, so also is spiritual wellness in a continual state of adjustment—sometimes advancing, sometimes weakening, but always alive. As is the case with most relationships, the deeper and longer we invest in our relationship with Christ, the fewer the dramatic, over-the-top instances occur to cause turmoil and questioning. Consider your walk with the Lord today versus when you first trusted Him. For new followers, the almost too-good-to-be-true belief in Christ's sacrifice and His intentions for our lives are beyond our comprehension. Ironically, a Christ follower who has known, experienced, and witnessed Christ's impact on his life and those around him for years oftentimes finds Christ's love and selfless sacrifice incomprehensible, but for different reasons—he or she has personally experienced it and their spiritual wellness has improved because of it.

The Beatitudes: the living characteristics that define you as one of His followers.

Wellness is a journey, not a destination. Face it—it's impossible to know everything about anything. Not *everything* about *everything*, just *everything* about *anything*! Somewhat discouraging, isn't it? Don't let it be! Rather let it stir you, challenge you, and motivate you to take your spiritual wellness journey to the next level . . . and the next . . . and the next. You'll most likely not commit the Bible to memory, but don't let that discourage you from becoming familiar with particularly relevant passages in your relationship with God. And about your prayer life—no formal setting required. A road trip, your kid's soccer game, or even the line at the DMV are marvelous venues to visit with the Lord.

The promise of spiritual perfection is not the goal this side of heaven, but that doesn't mean we shouldn't try to get as close as

possible. The Bible is full of commandments for believers to live sacrificially, and to be "salt and light" in the world. (For example, Matthew 6:19–24 and 5:13–16 .) When you work toward spiritual wellness on a day-by-day basis, even the slightest inroads you make in your personal ministry will cause the angels of heaven to rejoice. While you'll never achieve perfect spiritual wellness before arriving in heaven, you will inalterably change the course of your life and the lives of those you encounter, if you remain committed to pursuing spiritual wellness as you follow your Master Trainer, Jesus, the Christ.

Wellness is best defined relatively, and is therefore more personal and meaningful to each of us individually. I once heard a preacher tell his congregation, "God doesn't have any grandchildren." Think about how powerful that simple, succinct statement is and the conviction it carries with it. No one comes to the Lord through *anyone* except Jesus Christ. There are no second-generation believers in heaven, no genuine Christ-filled followers looking forward to an eternal dwelling with the Father who have not personally experienced Christ's transforming love and forgiveness.

And so it follows that each and every relationship with Christ is individual. Each believer's depth of knowledge, breadth of belief, and spiritual wellness are solely singular. We can empathize and sympathize with others on a deep level, but ultimately we are most intensely affected and changed by those experiences that happen to us and contribute to our spiritual selves. Oswald Chambers expressed it well: "The private relationship of worshipping God is the greatest essential element of spiritual fitness."[2]

But, the path to spiritual wellness with Jesus is not a solo sport. Our Leader does not expect us to grow spiritually without the help of others. Just as joining a running, cycling, or yoga group encourages and paces you to improve, in the same way, joining a group of Christ followers who seek to know, share, and multiply Christ in the lives of others will aid you in your quest for spiritual wellness. Your soul will do exercises on its own, but in a group you will do them better.

THE BOTTOM LINE

Our bottom line is that ultimately we have to define what spiritual and physical wellness is for each of us against God's clear revelation in Scripture. How we determine the parameters and establish the boundaries to live up to the benchmarks of biblical, spiritual wellness is a uniquely personal journey based upon our own educated, pondered, and prayed-over perspective. It is also based on the guidelines of those infinitely more schooled than ourselves in each area—be it those formally educated, professionally trained, and/or experientially learned. And, just as we get up before work to join a friend to jog or to join an exercise class, we do better when we are connected to a group of Christ followers who share our same goals for spiritual wellness.

Like the measures of physical wellness outlined by your vital signs, I want to point you to Jesus' measures of spiritual wellness outlined by the Beatitudes, the living characteristics that define you as one of His followers.

Despite the infinite amount of information, perspectives, and opinions available in all areas of wellness, several consistent themes evolve. For physical wellness, a balanced diet, a regular regimen of aerobic exercise, strength training, and flexibility postures, and a respectable amount of time spent in replenishment through sleep and relaxation are necessary components. In pursuit of spiritual wellness, a deepening relationship with God, experiential acts of service, and belonging to a community of fellow believers are essential elements. In the words of Kenneth Cooper, long regarded as the Father of Modern Aerobics and a zealous believer who keeps this whole pursuit of wellness in amazing perspective: "*Unless you are both spiritually and physically fit, you aren't truly fit.*"[3]

The Interrelatedness of Physical and Spiritual Wellness

Many physicians observe "the God factor" in patient prognosis and progress. If they already know and love Christ, then they have no trouble comprehending and crediting Christ with seemingly unexplainable medical miracles. If they don't enjoy a personal relationship with the Savior, it's a sure bet that within a year of receiving their coveted white coat, they'll witness more than just a few instances where the charts, scans, and lab results don't align with previous diagnoses. A tumor was once on a film and, now there is none. Where infection previously showed positive on a culture, it now reads negative. Or, where symptoms earlier were at a level of critical mass, they became dramatically reduced. It happens every day in hospitals across the country. The Great Physician heals and helps the hurting, physically and spiritually.

For the majority of us, however, the interrelatedness of our physical and spiritual well-being plays out in a much less dramatic setting than a surgical suite or a laboratory. The connection between the physical and spiritual can be realized in good times and bad. Consider the connection when we experience the runner's high and feel closer than ever to God and His creation as endorphins course through our veins. On the downside, we can also experience the complete lack of connectedness when depression takes hold of our lives and even the simplest tasks become overwhelming.

Respected physicians and researchers from some of our country's most noted and progressive institutions may not be able to explain the clinical relationship between body and soul, but they acknowledge this connection exists. The Mayo Clinic openly encourages patients to connect spiritually. In material designed to help ease patients' worries and concerns, the world-renowned facility says, "Certain tools to reduce stress are very tangible: exercising more, eating healthy foods and talking with friends. But there is another tool for helping you manage difficult times that can be just as beneficial, albeit harder to pin down—*embracing your spirituality.*"[4] Though the official stance avoids affiliation with any one belief system, it credits spirituality with helping "to give our lives context"—no small statement for a secular institution with an impeccable reputation.

Johns Hopkins University has gone so far as to produce a video entitled *Plans to Prosper—A Patient Guide to Faith and Health*, in which the researchers present five principles they consider to be vital in promoting good health. These principles encourage patients to: "trust God, clean house, give thanks, help others, and ask others and God for help." According to Medical Director of Clinical Research Jeanne McCauley, MD, "Recently, medical research has increasingly demonstrated that spirituality can be an important tool in helping you achieve health and wholeness. . . . There are many new studies that directly link patient spirituality to better overall health."[5] A world-class medical facility does not simply acknowledge a link between physical healing and spirituality but actually *embraces* it.

THOUGHTS PRECEDE EMOTION

As events come into our awareness, they may or may not become stressors that affect our physical, emotional, and spiritual wellness. Whether they become stressors depends on the interaction between the event, our personal history, beliefs, attitudes, and "emotional baggage." Don't worry—everyone has baggage! Each individual's baggage is the sum total of the beliefs and attitudes developed in response to past events in his or her life. Some baggage is useful—if you put your hand on a hot stove, it will burn you. Some baggage no longer serves a purpose—if I cross the street without holding someone's hand, I may be hit by a car. Many of us continue to hold on to emotional baggage long after it has served us.

Events that take place interact with our beliefs and attitudes and lead to automatic thoughts—the unconscious thoughts we have all day long. The majority of our thoughts tend to be negative simply because they try to help prepare us for whatever might happen to us. They also open us up to potentially distorted thoughts. Thoughts lead to emotions. Emotions are biochemical and physiological as well as thought-generated. These biochemical changes can lead to physiological changes that we call stress. They also work to produce behavioral responses.

Notice that thoughts precede emotions and emotions create biochemical changes in your body. This process sets up a cycle or loop in which your mind identifies the biochemical events and labels them as emotion. Certain biochemical changes may be identified as anger, sadness, happiness, or joy—but the point is that *thought precedes emotions.* Think peace-filled thoughts, experience peaceful emotions. Think angry thoughts, feel anger. Abraham Lincoln probably said it best, "Most people are about as happy as they make up their minds to be."

I tend to be very hard on myself. I remind myself often that I don't write as well as Philip Yancey. I don't cycle as fast as a Tour de France pro. I don't preach as well as T. D. Jakes, and I don't have a church as big as Bill Hybels. I know that the problem is I compare myself and my ministry to others rather than seek my identity in Christ, but I still do it. Somewhere along the way I learned to think less of myself by comparing myself to others in order to gauge how I was doing and ultimately who I was.

Several years ago a church member had an extra ticket to an event at Reunion Arena in Dallas and invited me to go with him. I often accept invitations like that in order to get to know the person in his world and build a relationship with him.

I had no real interest in the event. Speakers like Tony Robbins, Zig Ziglar, and Norman Schwarzkopf had been assembled to bring a message of positive thinking and "success" to those who gathered. I had never been to an event like that and, although I am a motivator as a preacher, I had always been a bit skeptical about those who sold hot air for a living. (Skeptics of organized religion had accused me of doing the same thing!) By the end of the morning, however, speaker after speaker demonstrated how my thinking affected not only my attitude but how I lived my life. I was convinced, and I left the event to retool my thinking about me, my relationships, and who I was as God's adopted son in Jesus Christ.

Since that event in the mid-1990s, my thinking—guided by God's Word, not my "self talk"—has changed dramatically. I still tend to compare myself to others and put myself down, but like refusing ice cream for raisins and walnuts for a snack, I now choose God's words and perspective about who I am and what I do. I live before the Audience of One and seek approval from the One who can say, "Well done, good and faithful servant." I know I could not have faced many challenges that have come my way without this new way of thinking.

Because we each have the ability to change our thoughts, we can change how we feel. Dr. Kenneth Cooper is emphatic in his belief about the relationship between our thoughts and our physical wellness: "If we have strong beliefs, along with discipline, we can reach a level of ultimate fitness both spiritually and physically. . . . The combination of both gives you a synergistic effect."[6]

He continues in his explanation by saying, "We have a wonderful way to improve our overall quality of life if we embrace the concept of fitness and wellness. We are meant to be active. We are challenged throughout the Bible that we need to consider our body as the temple of the Holy Spirit and treat it accordingly . . . If you believe you can improve your level of fitness, then you are going to do it. If you believe you can improve your spiritual life, then you are going to do it." Is it just me, or is anyone else hearing the chant of a determined little steam engine in the background . . . *"I think I can, I think I can, I think . . .*?

Who Is Spiritually Well? A Benchmark

The Beatitudes found in Matthew 5:3–10 are both a series of snapshots of Christlike life *and* a path to lead us to that life. Together, they form a benchmark for our spiritual maturity by helping us gauge our spiritual wellness as well as giving us a pattern for spiritual growth. They are Jesus' pattern for a new way of living in His kingdom.

Below is a brief composite of the traits of someone who is *living* the Beatitudes. Though by no means complete, you can see general tendencies and realize other complimentary characteristics of a Christ-filled follower.

Living the Beatitudes means you

1. are poor in spirit—	• are honest about your sins • recognize your spiritual poverty • are broken—not prideful—before God
2. mourn—	• grieve over your sinfulness • mourn the situations of others • receive and give comfort to others

3. are meek—	• are God-controlled rather than self-controlled
4. hunger and thirst for righteousness—	• want to be like Christ • are spiritually filled
5. are merciful—	• gladly receive God's mercy • show mercy to others
6. are pure in heart—	• seek purity in thoughts and deeds • see God at work around you
7. are peacemakers—	• seek to establish peace • apply God's peace to relationships and situations
8. are persecuted for righteousness—	• share Jesus' suffering • are aware of (concerned for) others' suffering • are disciplined without regard to consequences

Both individually and as a group, the Beatitudes depict a blessed life, a life favored by God. If someone asks you to describe spiritual wellness, you can point to the Beatitudes as the "vital signs" for spiritual health. These timeless spiritual truths constitute freeze-frame snapshots of the way God intended life to be.

A Blessed Life

As soon as I suggest that the Beatitudes picture the blessed life Christ intends for us, you ought to have a question. The root word from which we get *beatitude* means happy. And yet, how can being poor in spirit bring happiness? How can mourning picture happiness? In the answer to that question I believe we see one of the great secrets of spiritual health. The spiritually healthy person can deal with ambiguity.

Ambiguity means we cannot state with certainty some aspect of a matter. It means something can be understood in more than one way. Some things in life and in Scripture are absolutely clear and unambiguous, such as God's steadfast love. Other things, however, are much more difficult. Isaiah wrote, "'For my thoughts are not your thoughts, neither are your ways my ways,' declares the LORD" (Isaiah 55:8).

I once heard a theologian say that at the center of every central Christian doctrine is an apparent contradiction that cannot be resolved by human means. Is God one person or is God three persons? Was the incarnate Christ entirely God, or was He entirely human? Is God in absolute control, or has He granted human beings free will? The answer to each of those questions is yes; He has done both and is both.

Are you beginning to see what I mean? I have a friend who says life is a matter of staying out of the ditches. On most matters a person can go to extremes on either side of a spiritual truth. For example, we can overemphasize God's mercy and forget His judgment. The spiritually healthy person avoids those extremes. He or she has the ability to live with the ambiguity of life. Spiritual health like physical health requires maintaining balance.

It is my hope that as you grow in your understanding of the Beatitudes, you will tax your understanding to see how poverty can be blessedness, mourning can bring comfort, and how the other seeming contradictions create a *new way of living* for you. In that very effort God will stretch you and make you better able to see life His

> The spiritually healthy person can deal with ambiguity.

way. The ability to deal with the ambiguity of life and Scripture is a necessary practice of spiritual wellness. The Beatitudes represent portraits of the spiritually healthy person. By their nature they press us in the direction of spiritual maturity and set us upon the path to spiritual wellness.

Takeaway

On a trip to Hong Kong once, I saw a sign that read "Takeaway" over a café door. I did not know it meant the same as "Takeout" or "Carryout" back home. As soon as I found out what it meant, I felt at home! My wife and I "take away" some of our meals. I want you to have some "takeaway" you can carry with you after each chapter in this book, something you can chew on as you live out the life God has for you that day. I will also give you some questions to help you reflect on what you have read, which I hope will be an aid for the Holy Spirit to speak into your life.

So, here is your first morsel of "Takeaway" for your day.

God has created you as a whole person. Your physical, emotional, and spiritual natures are interconnected and affect each other. God has also revealed in Jesus' teachings that we call the Beatitudes a new way of living for those who trust Him. Your spiritual health is dependent upon whether or not you live as God prescribed. By trusting and following Jesus, you can change how you live and experience the life God created for you.

Questions for Reflection

1. What areas of your life are you holding back from fully releasing to God?

2. How have you personally experienced the connection between spiritual wellness and physical wellness? Do you see the connection once in a while or on a daily basis?

3. How would you describe what a soul is? Has this definition changed as you've grown in your spiritual walk?

4. Does it excite you or frustrate you when you realize that wellness, whether physical or spiritual, is an ongoing journey without a finite end?

5. Have you come to appreciate the ambiguity of the Beatitudes—namely, that the characteristics devalued by the world are those most closely associated with a life reflective of Christ's blessings?

CHAPTER 2

Becoming Spiritually Fit

Dear friend, I pray that you may enjoy good health and that all may go well with you, even as your soul is getting along well.

—3 John 2

I love to run. When I was 46, I began running seriously as part of a challenge by a church member to get in shape for what would be the race of my life. I had always run to stay in shape, but this goal required me to train longer and harder than ever before. I learned to cope with injuries, to pace my workouts, and to manage my energy and hydration on runs that lasted beyond five or six hours. Training for the "big" race enabled me to complete two "firsts" in my life—a marathon and, three weeks later, a 50-mile run. I have remained an avid distance runner and cyclist ever since. (I completed my tenth marathon, a trail marathon, in March 2012.)

As running became a central part of my lifestyle, I began to look differently at some of the biblical pictures of the Christian life. I concluded that the Apostle Paul was either an athlete or that he knew enough about athletics in order to carefully apply what a person learns in competition to his relationship with God. Our English words *gymnasium*, *stadium*, and *energy* come from Greek words Paul used to describe our relationship with

God. One athletic metaphor he used to describe growth in his relationship with Jesus is found in Philippians 3:13–16:

> *Brothers, I do not consider myself yet to have taken hold of it. But one thing I do: Forgetting what is behind and straining toward what is ahead, I press on toward the goal to win the prize for which God has called me heavenward in Christ Jesus. All of us who are mature should take such view of things. And if on some point you think differently, that too God will make clear to you. Only let us live up to what we have already attained.*

I picture a runner in the middle of a race who is single-mindedly pursuing the prize for the winner of the race. That is his "goal" in running the race. To "press on" is to pursue as a lioness pursues her prey or as one runner chases others to pass them. The "prize" in this case is Christ Jesus, and the "heavenward" call is God announcing the winner as the officials at the Olympic Games would announce the winners and their home countries.

Paul wrote that he was pressing on pursuing perfection, but in the Sermon on the Mount Jesus made an even more demanding statement, "Be perfect, therefore, as your heavenly Father is perfect" (Matthew 5:48). Don't despair at the call to perfection! While perfection seems like an impossible teaching, when you substitute the word *maturity*, the commandment seems more attainable. The word *perfect* in Matthew 5:48 is the same word for *mature* Paul used in Philippians 3:15. *Perfect* also means *complete.*

The Apostle Paul was a model of commitment. He confessed that he had not reached completeness but that he pursued it to take hold of it. Paul desired maturity and completeness in his relationship with Jesus. The kind of maturity and completeness he spoke of meant spiritual wellness and wholeness.

Don't despair at the call to perfection!

The goal of our growing Christian life is maturity in our relationship with Jesus. We are spiritually well and whole when we grow in becoming like Jesus in our daily life. As Paul so passionately said, being like Jesus is the *goal* and *prize* of the Christian life. While we cannot do this without God's help, it is helpful to understand that we can participate in the process of becoming like Jesus in the same way athletes train to enhance their physical skill—namely through consistency, gradual exertion, and calculated rest. Our goal is to become spiritually mature by pursuing a full and meaningful relationship with Christ and to graduate from a novice believer to a Christ-filled example of God's mercies and provisions for all who put forth the effort.

In his book, *Five Secrets of Living*, Warren Wiersbe explains the cause-and-effect relationship between growing in our relationship with the Lord and improving our physical health.

> The secret to remaining in God's presence is obeying His principles. The more we are obeying His principles out of love, the more we will want to spend time with Him and be in His presence. The more we are in His presence, the more we will experience love, joy, and peace. Being in His presence will give us more power, through the Holy Spirit, to make healthy choices and any necessary behavior changes. This, in turn, will impact our health in a positive way.[1]

To hear him explain it, you wonder why anyone would behave otherwise, but I know all too well how even the simple everyday tasks of life can interfere with the best laid plans when it comes to exercising. As committed as I am to honoring the Lord with my *temple*, I have done battle between the TV remote and my running shoes more times than I'd like to admit.

The obesity crisis facing our country tells me I am not alone in this classic good vs. evil conflict. Do any of these excuses sound familiar?

"Next commercial," we bargain for time.

"OK, maybe half-time . . . if it's not a close game," we rationalize.

"Well, what do ya know—it's already getting dark. Better get an earlier start . . . *tomorrow!*" we resolve.

Take heed my friend. Set the DVR and remember those wise words from Dr. Wiersbe the next time you're tempted to sit through the *Star Trek* marathon or the film *You've Got Mail* for the 14th time in lieu of lacing up the ol' sneakers. Spock and the Starship Enterprise can wait . . . your health and the opportunity to honor the Lord with your efforts to be healthy should not.

Blessings with a Promise

The Beatitudes provide the basis for how to love God with all our soul. However, before we go any further with Christ's exhortations to His followers, let's first explain the seeming paradox of being "blessed" and yet enduring unfavorable treatment and sufferings. Today, we toss the word *blessed* around so much and so casually its meaning is 180 degrees from how Christ originally intended it. As a result, the obvious contradiction in how many of us interpret the Beatitudes is completely understandable. Wrong, but understandable just the same.

R. T. France explains *blessed* this way:

> 'Blessed' is a misleading translation of [the Greek], which does not denote one who God blesses . . . but represents the Hebrew . . . 'fortunate', and is used . . . almost entirely in the format setting of a beatitude. It introduces someone who is to be congratulated, someone whose place in life is an enviable one. 'Happy' is better than 'blessed', but only if used not of a mental state but of a condition of life.[2]

Sounds infinitely more attractive when you fully grasp what Jesus promised in return for a life committed to living for Him, doesn't it? It's the hallmark of a loving and caring coach that tells you what is expected of you and then explains what you must do to succeed. In Christ, we see the Coach who cares deeply that we understand His lessons and lovingly longs for our success in developing a deep and intensely meaningful relationship with Him.

In the Sermon on the Mount Jesus taught about the kingdom of God. This was Jesus' first public teaching about the kingdom He came to establish. The Bible tells us that Jesus was teaching His closest followers when He saw a large crowd gathered on the side of a hill (Matthew 5:1–2). As He began to unpack kingdom life for them in His presence, Jesus pronounced how fortunate people with certain spiritual conditions were in His kingdom. Along with this announcement, He made them a promise—

several promises, in fact, for their future as His followers. This combination of pronouncements and promises make up the Beatitudes.

Look again at Jesus' words in Matthew 5:3–10:

> *Blessed are the poor in spirit, for theirs is the kingdom of heaven.*
>
> *Blessed are those who mourn, for they will be comforted.*
>
> *Blessed are the meek, for they will inherit the earth.*
>
> *Blessed are those who hunger and thirst for righteousness, for they will be filled.*
>
> *Blessed are the merciful, for they will be shown mercy.*
>
> *Blessed are the pure in heart, for they will see God.*
>
> *Blessed are the peacemakers, for they will be called sons of God.*
>
> *Blessed are those who are persecuted because of righteousness, for theirs is the kingdom of heaven.*

Stop reading and underline or circle the blessings you most relate to today. Do the same for the promises you most desire.

See how each of the verses is a promise for the future as well as an assurance for the present? Notice also how the first and last verse sort of bookend the other promises, presenting the ultimate in rewards—Christ's own kingdom. R. T. France continues,

> The beatitudes thus outline the attitudes of the true disciples, the one who has accepted the demands of

> God's kingdom . . . The tenses are future, except in the first and last, indicating that the best is yet to come, when God's kingdom is finally established and its subjects enter into their inheritance. But the present tense of vv. 3 and 10 warns us against an exclusively future interpretation. . . . The emphasis is not so much on time, present or future, as on the *certainty* that discipleship will not be in vain.[3]

Jesus identified the fortunate ones in His eyes and promised certain things that they would experience here and ultimately when He rules in the New Heaven and New Earth forever.

What the Beatitudes Are

The Beatitudes can serve as a benchmark for spiritual wellness and maturity. They illustrate what it means to love God with all our souls. To know whom Jesus blessed in His sermon is to know what kind of person Jesus wants us to become. Consider the following observations:

THE BEATITUDES REFLECT CONDITIONS OF THE HUMAN SOUL.
I believe Jesus saw the hearts of people when He looked out on the crowd that day. He saw their hearts and desires, and He chose to recognize them because of their needs.

The Beatitudes describe people who appear as unlikely candidates for the kingdom but who are actually blessed by God.

Remember, Jesus was announcing the "kingdom of heaven is near" (Matthew 3:2). He was describing the nature of kingdom people and their character. The people of Jesus' day had preconceived ideas about who was in the kingdom of God. They believed the wealthy, confident, and self-sufficient were blessed by God. They assumed all others must have been suffering because of sin or judgment in their lives (John 9:1–3). They, like us, assumed the superstars, successful, skinny, and beautiful people, are the blessed ones! More than 2,000 years after He first preached these words, the list of people Jesus blessed *still* doesn't match our preconceived ideas of who are "in" with God.

THE BEATITUDES REVEAL THE HEART OF GOD AND THE CHARACTER OF CHRIST.

John told us that Jesus is God revealed to us (John 1:18). The blessings are pieces of a puzzle that, when fit together as a whole, give us a picture of Jesus' heart. Each piece gives us insight into the person of Jesus, and together they give us a complete picture of the character of Jesus.

THE BEATITUDES ARE CHARACTERISTICS OF THOSE WHO FOLLOW JESUS.

While Jesus basically blessed the people present that day, I believe He also revealed the desired character of those who follow Him. These blessings form a list of characteristics that describe the character of those who follow Christ. Prior to the Sermon on the Mount and the presentation of the Beatitudes, Jesus told any and everyone that the kingdom of heaven was imminent and the time to repent—change your heart and mind—was now.

In explaining that "this discourse was intended for the nation of Israel," author Allen Ross characterizes the massive crowds that had gathered to hear Jesus' prophetic words as "the Israel of the future, the Israel that is hoped for," and "those who should repent and follow the king." Ross continues his explanation by rephrasing his perspective, "Jesus spoke to all the people of the true will of God, the righteousness that they must all exhibit if they repent and enter His kingdom, but which the disciples had already begun to perform. So the entire sermon is directed to all. And its theme is the righteousness that is the standard of his kingdom."[4]

What Jesus revealed to those in His presence more than 2,000 years ago and to those who follow Him today is one and the same, *and* it is the very basis for life with Him in His eternal kingdom. When we fully grasp the magnitude of Christ's words in this brief sermon, it suddenly becomes clear that to live like Christ truly is sacrificial from a worldly standpoint, but immeasurably glorious from an eternal viewpoint.

The Promise of the Exercises

When we parallel the discipline of following Christ against the discipline of pursuing physical fitness, several similarities present themselves: *Exercising is not the easiest path to pursue.*

Whether training for a 5K or delving into commentaries on a specific passage of Scripture, there is always something *easier* to do. The whole physiological explanation of why exercise is beneficial comes down to a simple principle—to make your muscles stronger, you've got to push them beyond their comfortable, sedentary state to the actual point of tearing them slightly. These microscopic tears then heal and leave the muscle stronger than it was before it was exerted. Done on a regular basis, this tear-recover-repair cycle grows and strengthens muscles perpetually.

This same principle is true for our spiritual growth. Every day that we spend in fellowship with God and His Word—learning more about His promises, the lives of the prophets, and the circumstances of His life—the closer we become to Christ. The important thing to remember in regard to growth and development physically and spiritually is that you have to *continually* adjust your exercises, intentionally going beyond what you have done before, whether it is adding more weight to your bicep curls or going deeper into learning the context of Jesus' words and wisdom.

The effect of exercising can be felt both short-term and long-term. If you've ever consistently followed a physical exercise plan, you know the cool down phase is usually the most enjoyable part of the workout. You've gone through your regimen, you're dripping sweat, and then the payoff: you get to stop! Seriously, the feeling of accomplishment when you've completed a round of circuit training or logged several miles on your running shoes should not be underestimated. You've done a job, presumably done it well, and now comes the time to enjoy the contentment of working hard.

On the flip side, the long-term benefit of exercising reveals itself in smaller, sometimes imperceptible ways such as being able to take the stairs without gasping for air, loading the SUV with cargo, or even being able to play just a little bit longer and stronger with the kids and grandkids. Dale Fletcher reminds us, "It is the intimate relationship with God accompanied with the resulting

> Spiritual exercise or disciplines must also be planned for in advance.

fruits of the Spirit that impact on us in such a way that will likely promote emotional and physical health. It all flows from knowing God and experiencing His mighty love."[5]

Spiritually, reading and praying through Scripture and spending a few moments of solitude in praise and adoration of God offers immediate calm and reassurance no matter our life situation. Long-term, stories of Christ's faithfulness and memory verses tucked within our hearts can be called upon whether your circumstances are celebratory or severe. Exercise, it appears, is truly the gift that keeps on giving.

The most significant payoff comes with consistency.
You can't do a few lunges across the room on Monday and a few more two weeks later and expect to see any real improvement. You'll stay sorer longer than you'll be stronger. You also can't commit John 3:16 to memory and hope for waves of comfort when the doctor says, "We need to talk." Just as any meaningful relationship requires the investment of time and effort, so does the relationship between you and your body and you and Christ. The formula is not rocket science. In fact, it comes down to the simplest of equations: put a little in, get a little out; put a lot in, have a lot to draw from. That, my friend, is math in its purest form.

SPIRITUAL EXERCISES

I once heard the principles that God reveals in the Bible described as spiritual exercises intended to help those of us claiming to be Christ followers to get into shape—spiritual shape, that is. And so it follows that if we are truly intent on shaping up, we should develop and commit to following a plan that helps us draw closer to that goal. I firmly believe that, like physical exercise, spiritual exercise or disciplines must also be planned for in advance, that it must become a priority at the expense of other commitments, and that it is one of the key components in a life well-lived.

Dallas Willard describes spiritual disciplines this way,

> The disciplines are activities of mind and body purposefully undertaken, to bring our personality and total being into effective cooperation with the divine order. They enable us more and more to live in a power that is, strictly speaking, beyond us, deriving from the spiritual realm itself, as we "yield ourselves to God, as those that are alive from the dead, and our members as instruments of righteousness unto God," as Romans 6:13 puts it.[6]

Part of any well developed exercise program pays attention to what is consumed. This is equally true physically and spiritually. Just as optimal health and fitness require a keen eye overseeing what we eat, spiritual health is also tremendously impacted by what we place in our heart, our mind, and our soul. When we want to know which foods are most beneficial regarding fitness, we turn to a nutritionist or other knowledgeable source. When we want to know which principles to follow in pursuit of spiritual wellness, there is no source more beneficial than Christ's own words—the Bible. Paul, for example, reminds us our thought diet should include, "Whatever is true, whatever is noble, whatever is right, whatever is pure, whatever is lovely, whatever is admirable—if anything is excellent or praiseworthy—think about such things" (Philippians 4:8).

Reading the Bible is just the beginning of learning and knowing the truth that will strengthen your understanding of Christ and His ways. Add time spent in prayer and you've upped your spiritual fitness level tenfold. Trust me when I say that nothing will take the place of surrendering your prayers of adoration, your appeals for forgiveness, and your pleas for Christ's intervention into your life like time spent seeking God's face and His active involvement in your life. If you're like most people, I think you'll find that this "peace that passes all understanding" (Philippians 4:7) will have residual effects on you physically. Your commitment to drawing closer to God will open your eyes to your opportunity to honor Him further with a healthy lifestyle that includes a balanced diet, a regular exercise routine, and a program of scheduled rest. It's that synergistic affect Kenneth Cooper referred to earlier, and it's a goal to pursue every day we draw breath.

The secret to living a life that best honors Christ and expresses the fruit of the Spirit (love, joy, peace, patience, kindness, goodness, faithfulness, gentleness, and self-control) is intentional in the exercises of our daily lives. By remaining in close contact with Christ on a moment-by-moment basis, the more motivated we are to behave honorably, and that ultimately translates into two more laps around the outfield or passing on the banana cream pie or turning off the TV in lieu of playing a game of kickball with our kids. Crazy, isn't it—kickball as a form of worship? But when your intent is to strengthen your heart's capacity, God will fill it to overflowing.

Chapter 2

A Pattern for Study

So now that we've established the link between physical and spiritual fitness and how spiritual exercises are to your soul what physical exercises are to your body, let me give you a preview of what to expect as we begin exploring each promise within the Beatitudes verse by verse. Most of us do well when we know what we're going to learn and how it is going to be presented. With this in mind, we will address each of the nine verses in the following manner:

- The People—*who* was Jesus blessing? Who were these "fortunate" ones? Why did He point out "the poor in spirit" and "those who mourn?" We want to know whom Jesus calls blessed; we want to try to understand what that condition looks like in our lives.

- The Characteristic—*what* is within each blessing? We want to know how Jesus exemplified this spiritual characteristic and whether any other part of the Bible describes this trait. We hope to discover the characteristics of spiritual wellness. We will discover how each trait builds upon the previous one and becomes the foundation for the next step toward the likeness of Jesus.
- The Promise—*what* promise did Jesus make in each category of those He blessed? We want to know what those promises meant to the first hearers and what they mean to us today. When Jesus promised the "pure in heart" would "see God," what did He mean? The answers to such questions will give us insight into how God empowers you to do what He calls you to do.
- The Illness—spiritual wellness implies the existence of a corresponding spiritual illness. For every condition Jesus

blessed, another condition may draw us away from God. Remember that wellness is always a matter of balance. For example, the meek may find themselves so afraid to hurt the feelings of others that they cannot make healthy decisions. We want to be aware of extremes that can lead to a downside rather than to full and meaningful relationships with Jesus and others.

- The Exercise—*what* can be done to enhance what God has begun to develop in your life? With each characteristic will be a suggestion for a spiritual discipline or exercise that will allow God's gift in you to grow. The exercise does not give the gift, but it can enhance it. For example, God will more effectively satisfy your hunger and thirst for righteousness as you follow the spiritual exercises of memorizing Scripture and observing a Sabbath.

A chart of this path and how we observe each of the Beatitudes is in appendix A in the back of the book.

Growing into His Likeness

I believe these characteristics build each upon another; one blessing is connected to the other as one's character develops into the likeness of Jesus. I see the first three characteristics (vv. 3–5), poor in spirit, mourning, and meekness, leading us to "hunger and thirst for righteousness" (v. 6). Once Jesus satisfies that hunger and thirst, the next three characteristics (vv. 7–9), mercy, purity of heart, and peacemaking, flow from being filled up with the righteousness of God. The last blessing (v. 10) is for those who are persecuted like the prophets and Jesus because they behave like Jesus, their Master.

Let me describe it to you this way. I like to run on trails rather than concrete. I try to fit in a trail run on almost every trip I take. These runs have become a metaphor for my life and spiritual growth. I once attended a conference in Denver with my staff. On the last morning of the conference, I got up very early and drove to Estes Park. I wound my way around the park until I came to the Deer Mountain Summit trailhead. I parked the car, prepared to run, and headed up the mountainside.

As I climbed, I realized I was not as acclimated as I thought I was. Altitude is a running flatlander's greatest enemy. Once my lungs and legs began to work properly, I was able to enjoy the trek up the trail. I reached the top in a short but challenging time. I found my way to the highest point on the ridge and looked out over the mountain range. The view was unbelievable. Snow-covered peaks formed a vista of power and glory. The sun splashed light on the mountains' faces, and I soon found myself singing praises to God and thanking Him for His beauty in creation and for His blessings in my life.

On that mountain I once again committed myself to go wherever God led me. Being with God on the mountaintop filled my soul with hope and grace. I wish time had permitted me to complete running the entire trail, but duty called me back. I made my descent to the car, meeting only a man and his son as they began their walk to the top. As I drove, the roads became wider and more crowded as I got closer to Denver, but I would not see the common tasks that faced me in the same way again. God touched my heart on that ridge. He changed me so that I was renewed to face the everyday tasks of ministry.

That trip to the mountain and return home is a metaphor for the trip we make with Jesus in the Beatitudes. Our journey with God is made up of valleys of common events punctuated by mountaintop experiences. I sense the same pattern of movement when I read the Beatitudes. See the course map below as a way to visualize what I mean:

The Journey We Will Take

Let me further describe something of the journey to a new way of living we will take through the Beatitudes:

- Everyday life exposes my poverty of spirit. Circumstances, choices, and others hold up the mirror to my inability to be the person I desire to be. My need draws me to begin my journey toward Christlikeness.
- Upon seeing my spiritual poverty, I mourn. I grieve because all my righteousness is as filthy rags (see Isaiah 64:6). I begin to sense the same brokenness in others as well, and I grow in my empathy toward them. Ironically, the pain of realizing how unlike Christ I am draws me farther up the mountain.
- In my brokenness I become willing to submit to God's leadership. For the first time, I experience genuine meekness, surrendering the personal power and gifts of my life to my Leader.

- The climb through poverty, grief, and submission makes me hungry and thirsty for the righteousness of God. I drink in and feast on God's righteousness as He invites me to the "table of inwardness." When I am satisfied that His righteousness completes my longing, God's promises draw me back down into the valley of life.
- Refreshed, I return to valley life with new purpose. I stop along the way to savor God's mercy, and God changes my heart. I no longer want to judge others. I want to show them the mercy God has shown me.
- I pause in my descent to see the panoramic beauty of God's creation. With a changed heart I see my relationships differently. I feel less need to impress others. My life becomes an integrated whole instead of conflicting parts. I can actually

see how God is working in my life and how all that happens fits into His purposes.

- Now that I am back in my routine on the valley floor, I find I want to bring the peace of God to others. I actively look for ways to make peace in the lives of others. The valley that exposed my poverty now is fertile with opportunities for bringing God's peace to others. I gain a reputation for being a "child of God."
- I learn that the more closely I follow Jesus, the more satanic powers push back and that sometimes I downright anger those I serve. In those times, I remember Jesus' words on the mountain, "Be glad and rejoice when you are persecuted for my name's sake for you are being treated just like all the others who bring my peace" (my interpretation).

You can see that the Beatitudes represent a path to a Christlike lifestyle, a new way of living for most of us. I want to encourage you to look at them in another way also. They are a plan for a day lived in the presence of God. There is much to learn as we contemplate the words of our Master Teacher/Coach. I believe we will find His blessings can fall on us as they did on that ancient hillside. My prayer is that with each chapter we will get a better grasp on what it means to love the Lord and live as He has designed for us to live.

Takeaway

The Beatitudes form a path we follow to a new way of living. They contain both a blessing and a promise experienced as we are in relationship with Jesus. Spiritual exercises or disciplines, like physical exercises, make it possible for us to experience what Jesus revealed in His message to His disciples. As you live in the valley of your relationships, God calls you to the summit of His presence, renews you, and sends you back into the valley to be His peacemaker.

Questions for Reflection

1, What does a blessed life look like to you?

2. How do you experience the kingdom of heaven here on earth?

3. Does it overwhelm you or challenge you to realize that the Beatitudes paint the picture of Christ's character and one that He desires for each of us? How so?

4. What can you do specifically to raise the bar on your exercise regimen—spiritually and/or physically?

CHAPTER 3

The Poor in Spirit

Blessed are the poor in spirit, for theirs is the kingdom of heaven.

— Matthew 5:3

I met Dave at a coffee shop. I could tell he was upset. We ordered our coffee and sat in a corner. I cut to the chase and asked, "What's going on? You said you had something to tell me."

He looked at his cup and gathered courage to speak. Then he whispered almost to himself, "My wife caught me."

"Caught you . . .?" I asked, trailing off to allow him the opportunity to complete the question.

"She caught me looking at pictures on the Internet," he answered with a red face.

"Wow," I said softly. "How did she respond?"

We spent the next hour talking about his habit of looking at inappropriate material on his computer. He came to confess to me because his accountability partners told him he needed to tell his pastor as a way to galvanize the process of repentance, reconciliation, and restoration.

About midway through the conversation he said, "I am so ashamed. How can I ever show my face at church again?" I told him he was doing the right thing and that his guilt was an appropriate response to his sin. I cautioned him, though, not to let his feelings prevent him from accepting God's forgiveness, freeing him from this behavior, restoring his marriage, and helping other men overcome the same habit. I said, "Your brokenness puts you right where God wants you to be, Dave. Jesus said, 'Congratulations to the poor in spirit, for they are perfect candidates for the kingdom of heaven!'"

For some of us, it takes such a devastating blow to self—ego, esteem, reputation—to realize our intense need for God. For others, we are awestruck by the magnitude of the sacrifice of Christ and are overwhelmed, almost beyond comprehension. Sadly, most of us operate in the dreadful lukewarm in-between. We hear of and intellectually understand the redemptive gift of Christ, but when it comes to accepting it on a personal level, more than a few of us do battle with demons, either from deeds long past or those that visit us on a much more current basis. Sure, we're sorry for our shortcomings and occasionally make temporary strides to move past them but, ultimately, our desires for the promise of a preferred future lose out to temptations of the moment or an unforgiving self-berating for past missteps. We hold total contempt for anyone as corrupt or debased as ourselves. That "Jesus thing"—forgiveness for *everything*—that works for *other* people, who haven't done the things that I've done, gone where I've gone, messed up like I've messed up.

> It takes such a devastating blow to self—ego, esteem, reputation—to realize our intense need for God.

Any of these thoughts sound familiar?

"Lord, I know You're in the business of forgiving, but I've

done some things I'd just as soon no one know about, if You know what I mean.

"I get how heaven's a place for all those people who've played by the rules their whole life, but there's one thing I'm not—and that's a rule follower."

"I can't forgive myself for half the things I've done, Lord. There's no way you can get past everything . . . remember my senior year? Remember the desperate years? Remember when I did whatever it took to make a buck?"

Ironically, it is because this kind of forgiveness is beyond the limits of our human comprehension and our limited personal abilities that we are unable to grasp God's complete and utter acceptance and forgiveness. If we can't forgive ourselves, we reason, then there's no way God can either. That kind of flawed logic, my friend, is the work of Satan and stands to come between
you and a relationship with Christ and eternity in heaven.

Suddenly, our battered and bruised self-image takes on a whole new level of significance when viewed through Christ's all-seeing, yet all-forgiving eyes. Because, you see, it is in this very recognition of worthlessness, this total disregard of self-value, this absence of *any* redeeming quality in which Christ Jesus does His most magnificent and transformative work. Christ wants nothing more than for His followers to acknowledge their need for Him and to follow Him completely. It's not a hall pass to a life free of challenges and obstacles, but it *is* an irrevocable ticket to eternity with the creator of the universe.

Why Start Here?

The journey of following Jesus begins in the valley of our relationships. There we experience the reality of life and realize that

God would always rather we come to Him mindful of our questionable service.

most of our dreams don't turn out like we dreamed them and people are not always who they seem to be in public. Circumstances, our choices, and the choices of others impact our lives in ways that help us realize we can't do this on our own, and we are not in control as we thought we were. The journey into the presence of God begins with the confession, "I need help!" It is only when we realize we are unbelievably unfit to stand before God and equally unable to honorably wear the title Christ follower without His help that we are in the most prime position to be used by and for God's will.

Undeniably the journey on the trail of spiritual growth and maturity will have its share of detours, challenging outside forces, and some seemingly insurmountable obstacles, but for those who continue to put one foot in front of the other and focus their hearts, heads, and hands heavenward, the view from the summit is beyond description. To be used by and for God's work throughout our days on earth is a mountaintop experience no matter where you're standing.

Commentators who have long studied the powerful words of the Beatitudes agree upon several points concerning this introductory statement:

- It is the cornerstone upon which the other verses rest, the root from which the other verses grow; as a result, its placement as the first of a series of characteristics God desires is intentional;
- It represents an emptying of oneself whereas the rest speak of a filling. This emptying must take place before one can then be filled to overflowing with Christ's unsurpassed love;

- Being "poor in spirit" is a picture of someone turning to God out of total despair;
- Being "poor in spirit" does not reflect a person's status or financial standing, nor is it a suppression of personality, drive, enthusiasm, or motivation, but rather a reflection of the heart.

Two Biblical Examples

When I look to the Bible for who best illustrates what it means to be "poor in spirit," I am immediately struck by two examples from Scripture—Moses and a tax collector Jesus observed. Consider first Moses, a humble servant who ultimately became the self-sacrificing leader of the Jews who respectfully, but fervently, questioned God when asked to lead an exodus of God's chosen people out of bondage. Read the following exchange and see if you can't help but empathize with Moses and his feelings of self-doubt and self-worth.

> *The Lord said, . . . "So now, go. I am sending you to Pharaoh to bring my people the Israelites out of Egypt." But Moses said to God, "Who am I, that I should go to Pharaoh and bring the Israelites out of Egypt?" . . . "O Lord, I have never been eloquent, neither in the past nor since you have spoken to your servant. I am slow of speech and tongue."*
>
> —EXODUS 3:7, 10–11; 4:10

Here God picks Moses not just as His first-round draft choice but as the captain of the team, and all Moses can do is mumble and stumble around, offering up reasons why he isn't the man for the job. Can't you see him slightly kicking at the dirt, head hung low, grumbling under his breath at what God has asked him to do? To his credit, however, Moses was humble in his self-doubt rather than boisterous in his borderline abilities. God would always rather we come to Him mindful of our questionable service to Him rather than boldly proclaiming how *we* might benefit *Him!*

The biggest issue that Moses failed to recognize was that God wouldn't call him to serve in *any* capacity—big, bigger, or monumental— without first equipping him to do so. Centuries later, that same promise holds wondrously true for us also. Like my friend Dave, Moses didn't feel up to the challenge before him but, in reality, both men were just where the Lord would have them to be to use them most effectively—aware of their total dependence upon Him for any chance of moving forward.

My second example is more like a before and after picture of God's transcending love and the humility of spirit it brings with it. Read the following passage that illustrates the parable of the Pharisee and the tax collector found in Luke 18:9–14:

> *To some who were confident of their own righteousness and looked down on everybody else, Jesus told this parable: "Two men went up to the temple to pray, one a Pharisee and the other a tax collector. The Pharisee stood up and prayed about himself: 'God, I thank you that I am not like other men—robbers, evildoers, adulterers—or even like this tax collector. I fast twice a week and give a tenth of all I get.'*
>
> *"But the tax collector stood at a distance. He would not even look up to heaven, but beat his breast and said, 'God, have mercy on me, a sinner.'*

> *"I tell you that this man, rather than the other, went home justified before God. For everyone who exalts himself will be humbled, and he who humbles himself will be exalted."*

This is an example of a man who was confident of his own righteousness to the point of looking down on anyone not equal to him socially, and the story of a man, who by trade was feared and hated, but was able to see what the other man couldn't—his complete worthlessness apart from God. What was the result of the prayers of these two men? According to Jesus, the Pharisee went home condemned, while the tax collector went home justified.

Only the poor in spirit will enter into the kingdom of God because they come to God with full knowledge of their own brokenness and readily confess it to God. They realize they are unfit for residence in the kingdom of God, and yet they graciously accept that it is theirs upon accepting Christ into their life.

Let's take our first step on the trail to spiritual wellness. What did Jesus teach us, and what does this look like in everyday life? We will follow our pattern of study for each of the Beatitudes we outlined in the last chapter. Let's go!

> It's human "I-can-do-it-myself" nature.

The People

For all the self-help books; self-improvement tapes; and think-yourself-rich, or -thin, or successful-arena-filling, once-in-a-lifetime seminars across the country, you'd think personal fulfillment and the realization of our individual goals were nothing more than a $14.99 paperback away.

Trouble in your marriage? Read *this*.

Career falling off the tracks? Listen to *these* CDs.

Want to know the *real* meaning of personal happiness? Send the first of "three easy installments" to Success Seminars International before midnight tonight . . . operators are standing by.

You bet they are.

Seriously? To read the back-cover copy of some of these so-called answer books or hear the snappy sales pitch of the television or radio announcer touting these "be all/do it all/have it all" prosperity seminars, you'd be crazy to pass on such an offer. But answer this—if self-actualization, confidence in oneself and one's abilities, and an understanding of how "to win

at life" *really* were just a few lectures and lessons away, why is it that Americans are turning to prescription antidepressants, legalized self-medicating solutions (like alcohol), and illegal, mind-blowing substances in record numbers?

I'll tell you why.

As a pastor who's counseled hundreds of people through chemical dependencies, emotional rough spots, and life-altering pronouncements (think: "*You're fired*," or "*I'm leaving you*," or "*The tumor is malignant*"), the answer to me is obvious: they've become *poor in spirit*. They are void of any true hope for positive change, and they haven't found comfort in the welcoming and waiting arms of the Lord. It's not hard to understand. It's human "I-can-do-it-myself" nature and, if it doesn't kill you, it'll surely make your life miserable.

The glorious, almost too-good-to-be-true truth is that it doesn't have to be this way. There is another way to live.

Jesus began His message by saying, "*Blessed are the poor in spirit, for theirs is the kingdom of heaven*" (Matthew 5:3). He announced that the poor in spirit are blessed of God; the kingdom of heaven belongs to them! What was He teaching us about kingdom people and spiritual wellness? Who are these people? The obvious answer is the people who gathered to hear His message. Jesus looked over the crowd and blessed those who were potentially people of His kingdom. He blessed them to encourage them to follow Him. He blessed them to teach His disciples the kind of people who belong to Him. He blessed them and promised a response by God to their spiritual condition.

Blessed in the Beatitudes means *happy, fortunate, highly favored by God*. Be careful, however, not to interpret Jesus' words as instructions regarding what to do to *find* happiness. *Blessed* means so much more than our limited concept of happiness. Jesus was not talking to his audience about how they felt that day or how they measured up to some definition of happiness in their culture. Jesus was telling them *how* God saw them and *why* He would show them His favor. Get this extremely important perspective about Jesus' words: *The Beatitudes are Jesus' revelation of God's perspective on life, not an affirmation of our spiritual condition*. Jesus was not stating His approval of our current condition as the way we should remain. He declared God's favor on those who *recognize* their condition, those He saw as "poor in spirit."

Jesus blessed those who realized their need for God. He called them "fortunate." Whatever more Jesus meant, He congratulated those who were honest about their poverty of soul.

Jesus looked over the crowd and blessed those who saw themselves as unworthy of God's blessing. They knew they were not kingdom people. That may have been the very reason they sought out Jesus that day. Like Dave in the opening story, these people were so aware of their sinfulness, they had lost any sense that God would even want to love them. I believe Jesus blessed these people because they were positioned spiritually to receive both God's forgiveness and His leadership to change their lives.

I can just imagine what you're thinking now, "That's all well and good for those poor followers standing on the hillside that day, but what does the poor in spirit look like to me in the twenty-first century?" Surprisingly, it doesn't look that much different. Sure, we dress a bit different, we can nuke our coffee when it gets cold, and we can send a live video feed halfway across the world from our personal computer, but when it comes to the human condition, we're not too terribly far removed from those people who lived in Jesus' day. Just because the men wore tunics not unlike dresses and they didn't pass the time talking about V6 versus V8 motors doesn't mean they didn't have many of the same concerns and inner dialogues we have today.

They wanted to be happy in their relationships and to do what was best for their families.

They wanted to be successful in their business dealings.

They wanted to be respected while on earth and to have made a positive difference when they were gone.

In short, they wanted what most of us want whether we're 25 or 95, living in Dallas or Dubai, turning a wrench, teaching a class, or making deals for a living—they wanted the supernatural peace that comes from following God. But that only happens when first we admit our negligent behaviors, our obstinate tendencies, and our total unworthiness before the sacred throne of Christ. We would do well to learn from their collective example of what it meant then and what it still means today to be poor in spirit.

Then as now, certain characteristics are present in the lives of those who could best be described as "poor in spirit." These are individuals who do not see themselves as the answer to all their problems. Jesus challenged the self-sufficiency of the religious leaders of His day and offered God's favor to those who admitted their inability to solve the sin problem by themselves.

The poor in spirit realize they have drained their spiritual bank accounts and cannot pay their spiritual debts. They know they are spiritually broken before God. In earthly terms, think of it as someone who has maxed out their spiritual credit cards—*all* of their credit cards. They didn't set out to do so, but they got behind on this bill, skipped that one, and spent well beyond their means. For a while, they were able to keep their creditors at bay, making minimum payments, but as the balances increased and the interest rates skyrocketed, it soon became impossible even to send *some* of their creditors *some* of the money they were owed.

In desperation, they call their lenders and beg for mercy—asking for a reduced interest rate, an extended grace period, or even a pennies-on-the-dollar payment settlement—anything that will save them from the total declaration of bankruptcy. They know and the lenders realize that, short of some concession on the part of those to whom so much is owed, the inevitable fate for those overextended is perpetual indebtedness. In short, the debtors are simply in too deep to ever recover without intervention.

> Humility is the foundation for every characteristic of a disciple.

The poor in spirit may have vastly different backgrounds and strikingly different roads to redemption, but they are one and the same when at last they realize the intensity of their need, the depth of their debt, in light of the saving grace of Christ. They bend their knees to God and confess their unworthiness before Him. Sincerity of soul was all Jesus wanted when He first spoke these words, and it's still all he asks of us today. He blessed those like the Pharisee who did not come to Him performing religious activity as a way to earn God's love but rather in humble humility like the tax collector we talked about earlier. William Barclay summarized the meaning of poor in spirit this way, "Blessed is the man who has realized his own utter helplessness, and who has put his whole trust in God."[1]

As the ultimate example, Jesus in no way lacked anything in spirit yet, to the point of a tortuous death, He exemplified a life void of spiritual pride. Instead, Christ displayed unwavering humility, both to those who worshipped Him and those who ridiculed Him. This was because He drew His strength from His intense spiritual need to remain in fellowship with the Father—a lesson it would benefit all of us to learn and actively practice. You see, when you acknowledge a spiritual need within your life, it usually leads to humility of self. Humility is the foundation for *every* characteristic of a disciple. Followers of Christ accept that righteousness comes only from God. We cannot find our way into God's favor by keeping the law, but we must trust "a righteousness from God . . . (that) comes through faith in Jesus Christ to all who believe" (Romans 3:21–22).

Followers of Jesus know that God confounds conventional wisdom and chooses the spiritually poor to inherit the kingdom of heaven (James 2:5). Apprentices of the Christ hear the words of Jesus and respect those who find themselves in spiritual poverty because their Leader has blessed such people. They are part of Christ's kingdom if they accept God's provision for them.

Poverty of spirit also allows us to understand that our strength is from God. Paul confessed he had a nagging problem in his life, "To keep me from becoming conceited because of these surpassingly great revelations, there was given me a thorn in my flesh, a messenger of Satan, to torment me. Three times I pleaded with the Lord to take it away from me" (2 Corinthians 12:7–8). You can almost sense his frustration over the fact that, from his perspective, he asked God to remove his ailment so he could better serve God (or so he thought). God's answer to him was, "My grace is sufficient to you, for my power is made perfect in weakness" (2 Corinthians 12:9). This response by God to Paul's confession of weakness allowed the apostle to say, "Therefore I will boast all the more gladly about my weaknesses, so that Christ's power may rest on me" (v. 9). Paul's weakness became the basis for God's continued mighty work through his life.

Jesus calls you favored by God when you are poor in spirit because in that condition God can be your only source of strength. That is why the kingdom of heaven will be yours!

The Promise

Jesus blessed the poor in spirit "for theirs is the kingdom of heaven" (Matthew 5:3). Jesus announced that those who were poor in spirit belonged to His kingdom. As He launched His public ministry to establish the kingdom of God on earth, He identified those who would be in it. The kingdom of heaven Jesus spoke of is both the rule of Christ in a person's heart and His reigning presence in the world. This kingdom is both present and future, but we only experience it in relationship with Jesus Christ. Those who are citizens of heaven (Philippians 3:20) have been sent to serve others in the name of Jesus in order to get a taste of God's desires "on earth as it is in heaven" (Matthew 6:10).

Jesus' message from the beginning of His public ministry was, "Repent, for the kingdom of heaven is near" (Matthew 4:17). He announced that God's purposes were found in Him. His entire ministry was about trusting Him to be the King and Messiah of God's people and bringing people into the kingdom of God. I don't want to oversimplify an important New Testament idea, but the easiest way to think of the kingdom of heaven is *both* as your relationship with Jesus and your disciple-like lifestyle now *and* as a reality in eternity later.

This now and later, two-dimensional promise regarding the kingdom of heaven makes me think of some of our past family vacations. We would determine where we wanted to go and then begin making arrangements to get there. Wherever it was—the mountains, the beach, or just about anywhere outside the city limits—it was what the leadership gurus characterize as "a preferred end," which was speaker talk for someplace we wanted to go and, therefore, were willing to sacrifice to get there. In anticipation of our trips, we'd forgo present-day indulgences in lieu of hoped-for treats. We'd read about our destination, make any necessary prepayments, and envision ourselves already there.

You know what I learned from all the pre-vacation excitement preparation and planning? I learned that no slick, trifold brochure could do justice to the grandeur of the Rocky Mountains. No video set to the melody of steel drums could evoke the power of a breathtaking sunset against the ocean. Even stories of people who had travelled where I wanted to go and returned couldn't quite take the place of actually being there myself. In a crazy and oversimplified kind of way, that's how I see the blessed promise of heaven. Sure, we're to do anything and everything we can *today* to prepare for our eventual arrival, all the while excitedly anticipating our glorious, prepaid accommodations!

Jesus' promise to His first hearers applies both to our eternal condition and our present lifestyles. As we confess our poverty of spirit, God provides the gift of eternal life as we embrace Him in faith. To confess our sin (poverty of spirit before holy God) and to trust Jesus as risen Lord (Romans 10:9–10) is to receive the promise of kingdom membership. Eternal life in heaven comes through a trust relationship with Christ (1 Peter 1:3–5), and eternal life begins now, not after we die. God truly blesses us when we receive our gifts!

The Illness

Detours and dangerous obstacles crowd the journey toward spiritual health. We want to be aware of these potentially damaging conditions as we follow the path to spiritual maturity. Remember that health always means balance. When taken to an extreme, even the characteristics called the Beatitudes can each become destructive.

You can easily see how poverty of spirit can lead to spiritual illness if pushed to the edge. The prophet Elijah became afraid of Jezebel's threats to kill him after a particularly powerful confrontation with the prophets of Baal on Mount Carmel

(1 Kings 18). The result: Elijah fled into the wilderness, confessing his inability to go on. He knew that he was no match for Queen Jezebel's anger and cunning mind. He certainly had a form of spiritual poverty, but his spiritual condition did not lead to his acting like a man of God. Instead, it caused him to run and hide.

Poverty of soul can cause you to run from spiritual challenges. It may force you into a wilderness experience that leads you to say like Elijah, "I have had enough, LORD. . . . Take my life" (1 Kings 19:4).

When we realize we are poor in spirit, we have three choices: we can choose to try harder in our own strength, we can give up, or we can allow God to take over and lead us. The first choice eventually leads to exhaustion, just as it did for Elijah. When we turn to seeking solutions by our own efforts and those don't help, we often run away or lose confidence in God.

God's plan for spiritual poverty does not mean defeat. Running away or giving up are our selfish reactions to things we cannot control. To accept your spiritual poverty as the basis for God to work in your life is the sign of spiritual wellness. Because being poor in spirit brings you to the place of exhausting all of your own resources, God can then work powerfully in you through His Word, Spirit, and Church. Then you can trust God to be your source of strength. You can confess with Paul, "when I am weak, then I am strong" (2 Corinthians 12:10).

The Exercises

This new way of living means making room in your life for God to lead. The question then becomes, *how can you make such room?* Spiritual exercises, or disciplines, help this to happen. As I wrote in a previous book, *My Identity in Christ*, "Spiritual disciplines are like practice. They do not create the gift. They simply enhance the gift God has given you through His grace." Spiritual exercises can translate into disciplines for your body, mind, and soul as you allow God's presence and purposes to become more vital realities in your life. They provide practice in following Jesus in real-life situations. You make spiritual exercises part of your life just as you incorporate physical exercise and healthy food choices. They are designed to make healthy and whole that which God created.

Let me suggest two separate but related disciplines that God can use powerfully to work in your life. Not accidentally, both come from Elijah's experience—*solitude and silence.*

Elijah did not intentionally choose solitude and silence as spiritual disciplines. (Remember, he was running away from challenges and whining to God about his circumstances.) What God did in those settings, however, is an example of what God can do in us if we intentionally choose to go where Elijah went.

Elijah first found solitude. By running to the wilderness and then retreating 40 days and nights to Mount Horeb, Elijah removed himself from his life's circumstances (1 Kings 19:6–9). He removed himself from the distractions of spiritual battles and physical threats. On the mountain of solitude he experienced God in ways he never expected.

As a spiritual exercise, solitude enhances your sense of spiritual poverty. When you take yourself out of the frustrations and challenges of life, you get a true reading of your spiritual condition. Being alone allows you to hear your soul. This can be a frightening experience if you are not familiar with the sounds your heart and soul make. Solitude forces you to be with yourself in all of your hurts, sin, and inadequacies. Rather than covering those up with entertainment and activity, you can confess them to your loving Father. Without a place to be alone with God, you may never know the true condition of your soul. I encourage you to be patient in this particular pursuit because, even in the absence of traditional distractions such as work demands, family responsibilities, and social obligations, it takes a conscious effort not to seek out or fall subject to newfound distractions.

Let me give you an example. Let's say you've cleared your work schedule, told the family of your intentions, bowed out of the PTA committee meeting this week, and borrowed a friend's lake cabin for a few days. Ah, the expectations that fill your mind as you look forward to the break from the daily grind. The hours of prayer, the hours of reading, the hours free to focus on God.

You say your good-byes and hit the road, channel surfing the radio looking for golden oldies from the 1980s. You're belting it out with Hall and Oates when conviction strikes . . . you could be using this drive time to wind down and prepare for your sabbatical of soul. You click the radio off. Mile marker 328 . . . 329 . . . 330 . . . *Arghhhh!* The silence is deafening. You've caved to the top 40 countdown after praying all of 84 seconds!

You arrive at the cabin still humming the catchy refrain from "Xanadu" and breathe in the country air. After settling in, you tell yourself it's time to get down to business. Genesis 1: "In the beginning." This is not quite the spiritual awakening you had in mind and besides, the wind keeps blowing that loose shutter on the east side. You find a hammer, but no nails to tack it back up, but not to worry, you remember seeing a Home Depot not far off the exit you took off the interstate. Three hours later, the shutter has been nailed into submission and is silent. The sun has set and you decide to call it an early night because tomorrow . . . well, tomorrow, you're *really* going to get after this spiritual journey.

See what I mean. Good intentions. High hopes. Even in a conducive setting. Be warned, my friend, that seeking solitude is a daunting task. In fact, most of the time the physical setting is a distant second to the other preparations we make to be alone with God.

Richard Foster reminds us, "Solitude is more a state of mind and heart than it is a place."[2] You don't have to go into the desert and find a cave as the prophet did to practice this exercise. You can practice solitude every day. I heard a simple formula at a leadership conference several years ago that gave me a program of solitude for my life. The seminar leader told us to, "Divert daily. Withdraw weekly. Quit quarterly and abandon annually." This pattern of stepping out of the rush of life allows you to hear your heart. These moments also allow God to serve you in your weakness if you allow Him to.

Solitude invites silence. Silence follows you to your place away from the noise of life. Silence is how you hear God. When God revealed Himself to His prophet, He was not in a powerful wind, earthquake, or fire. Elijah expected God to be in these noisy, powerful experiences, but God revealed Himself to Elijah in "a still small voice" (1 Kings 19:12 KJV). God did not speak from the noise of nature or man's creation. God spoke from silence in a "gentle whisper" (v. 12 NIV). When the prophet heard the silent voice of God, he stepped out of his quiet place and spoke with the One who called him.

Noise is everywhere. Even as I type these words in my quiet office, I hear the hum of the computer fan and the room's florescent lights. Add to that the conversation in the outer offices and hallways and the sound of cars on the street outside my window, and you can understand why it is hard to hear the "still small voice" of God.

Just as it is challenging to seek solitude, it can also be a daunting task to engage in silence. I've learned that silence is an incredibly valuable commodity in my life, and I take any and every opportunity I have to walk in silence for however brief the moment is—a quick trip to pick up dinner at the Chinese takeout is just enough to praise my Father for the immediate blessings of the day. My daily run (without earbuds) affords me a longer stretch of time to revel in the progression of the seasons and God's orderly and provisional timetable. Even the seclusion of my shower provides a few moments of ceramic tile acoustics to belt out some of my favorite hymns (without the disapproving glances of my family!).

It's frequently not easy to seek out and practice solitude and silence, but I'm confident the Lord honors our efforts to put aside the details that crowd and cloud our daily lives long enough to give Him our undivided attention. Just as we don't like it when someone continues reading the newspaper or watching television or texting their BFF while we try to talk with them, Jesus doesn't like coming in second to the likes of a *Seinfeld* rerun.

To follow Jesus is to follow Him to quiet places. Luke wrote of a praying Savior who found both solitude and silence in the hills around Him (Luke 6:12, for example). God the Father spoke clearly to Jesus in the silence of a mountaintop experience (see

Luke 9:28–36). Jesus exercised solitude and silence in His life to stay on mission with the One who sent Him.

The poor in spirit do not fear solitude and silence. They seek it out, for there they hear the voice of God.

Takeaway

We're not really going to make lifestyle changes without first realizing that we are not the answer to our own problems. Poverty of spirit is an issue of God's power rather than willpower. Jesus congratulates you if you realize and confess your poverty of soul. You are ready to be part of His kingdom when you are in that condition. This new way of living calls you to find quiet places to listen to your soul and hear God's voice answer its cries. You will find that in your weakness you will experience God's strength that will move you to the next step of spiritual health.

Questions for Reflection

1. Do you know of someone personally who lives a life poor in spirit? What traits in that life reflect Christ's love and rule?

2. Can you identify with Moses' self-doubts about his ability to do as God directs him?

3. The Beatitudes speak of the promise of heaven now and later. Can you think of other life experiences that bring hope for now as well as later?

4. Have you intentionally experienced solitude and silence (as Elijah did unintentionally) in an effort to better hear God's voice speak to you? What was that experience like?

CHAPTER 4

Those Who Mourn

Blessed are those who mourn, for they will be comforted.

—Matthew 5:4

I knew all too well the voice at the other end of the phone. Between the sobs and the choppy, near hysterical description of a barroom fight, I instinctively knew it was Debbie. She was mother to Scott, a young man in our church who was chronically in trouble. Through the years I'd watched Scott grow from awkward and insecure preteen to tough and troubled teenager and now an angry and volatile young man entering adulthood. I'd also watched as his misdeeds escalated from boyhood mischief to misdemeanors to more serious crimes that eventually landed him in prison briefly.

This time, however, the call from the police wasn't about street racing. Or shoplifting. Or drug possession. This time it was worse. This time it was her son. In the hospital. Fighting for his life.

Debbie wept and I listened until her sobs subsided and she was able to speak a bit more coherently. Little by little she described the incident that had landed Scott in the hospital, listed in critical condition and not completely aware of what had happened to him. She knew there had been fights before;

Scott just seemed to bring that out in people. But in the past, he'd gotten out with no more than a black eye or a busted lip. Nothing had ever escalated to this level.

When she finished replaying the account the cops had told her, we prayed long and hard over the phone—first, for Scott's complete physical recovery, but also his emotional maturity and for some root of a spiritual life to take hold. As our conversation wound down, I promised to see Debbie the next day at the hospital when I came to visit Scott. She rushed to tell me one more thing before I hung up: despite the seemingly contrary circumstances, she knew in her heart her son had changed for the significantly better, to the point where he wanted his life to *really* count for something.

The bittersweet irony of Scott's dire condition up against

what his mother had said wasn't lost on me. Though I had never ended up in the hospital due to a run-in with another guy's fist, I had found myself in *critical* condition many times before in ways that ran contrary to where I, too, had said I wanted to be. Scott wasn't unique in his vast departure from where he wanted to be, and neither was I. The difference, however, between our two journeys was that I had come to the mind-blowingly humble acknowledgement that I couldn't get to where I was going on my own; I *had* to have Christ. Scott was still fighting his demons, but the constant beep-beep-beep of the heart monitor beside him was about to serve as a literal wake-up call to the mangled mess of a young man in the hospital bed.

Scott and I visited for quite a long time the next day. We talked about his injuries, his prognosis, and his takeaway from this incident. I encouraged him and challenged his conviction to turn his life around, and he promised to give serious thought to my suggestions.

We kept Scott on the prayer list at church that week and his condition was eventually upgraded to stable by week's end. Debbie felt comfortable enough to leave his bedside and I saw her the following Sunday as she came to pray during the response time of our worship service. I stepped down to join her and, as we knelt on the steps together, she began telling me how disfigured her son's face still was and would be for quite some time. Her eyes were filled with tears as she said, "His face is so swollen, you can hardly recognize him. But yesterday when I looked at him, something was different; a peace came over me. I suddenly realized Jesus must have looked like that when he died on the cross *for me*." She paused and then added, "I confessed that Jesus died for Scott, and I felt a peace that all this would work out according to God's plan."

It was at that very moment, as a mother mourning over the consequences of her son's sin that she became the living embodiment of what Christ meant when He said, "Blessed are those who mourn, for they will be comforted" (Matthew 5:4).

The People

Some interpretations of *blessed* equate the word to *being happy* or in a *state of happiness*. And it is generally agreed that someone who *mourns* is in a decidedly *un*happy state of mind. So following this train of thought, it would stand to reason that you could read this verse as, "Happy are the unhappy!" and, as counterintuitive as this sounds at first, it *really* is what Jesus meant. But, our natural inclination is not to pursue unhappiness in *any* venue or under *any* circumstances. In fact, our culture today promotes

> True happiness can be found in sorrow.

going to extreme measures to find and secure that constantly moving, always elusive, and ever-changing destination we call *happiness*.

Consider the following appeals the media and society constantly put before us.

Spouse let you down? Tired of the ol' "commitment scene"? A no-fault divorce is just a phone call away.

Got a few too many grape juice stains on the ol' couch? Finance your way to a whole houseful of furniture and don't even think about making a payment for any of it this side of five years.

Or maybe your minivan with the duct-taped bumper just isn't promoting the image you feel you deserve . . . you know, the *real* you. For as little as a couple of hundred dollars and your signature, you could change that homely image and be cruising the town in style within the hour.

Whatever terms we use to describe our station in life, there's always a billboard or a 30-second radio spot or a slick magazine cover telling us we could do better, prosper more, and yes, wait for it . . . *be happier* than we are today if only . . .

Ah, happiness . . . we worship at the altar of your sculpted abs, pristine furniture, and shiny hubcaps.

And yet, Jesus tells us that not only is true happiness *not* found in these things but that it can be found in sorrow. Gut-wrenching, woe-is-me, self-abasing *sorrow*. Jesus blessed those who had lost their innocence and self-respect—people who mourned the condition of their lives. In light of their desires and what the world offered as happiness, they had come to the place of sorrow rather than what they thought they had been promised.

This reality applies to us individually, and it applies to those of us who grieve for the sins of others. That is why Debbie was such an accurate portrayal of this verse. She knew that regardless of the claims Scott had made about turning his life around, his actions said otherwise and that until he personally mourned for who he had become and the lifestyle he had chosen, the cycle of bad behavior would continue. For Scott, for Debbie, for me, and for you, it takes each of us getting to a point of desperation, crying out for salvation, and realizing our dire need for more than we alone can provide. Once we arrive at the point of conviction and confession, then we can graciously and humbly embrace Christ's offer of redemption.

In light of the progression of the Beatitudes, once we realize our poverty of spirit, we are led to mourn over the condition of our souls and the spiritual condition of others. Jesus then blesses those who confess their spiritual bankruptcy, who are convicted of sin, and who are willing to follow Him. And the promise He makes in return for a sobering admission and acknowledged need? He promises comfort beyond our grasp from the God on Most High.

The Characteristic

What does it mean to *mourn* in respect to spiritual wellness? Because Jesus was perfect in every way (Hebrews 4:14–16), He had no need to mourn for Himself. However, by His very nature He mourned over the sins of others because He realized the great chasm of

Jesus wanted to touch and transform.

separation sin created between man and God. Further into the Gospel of Matthew, Jesus travels from village to village to share the good news of salvation through Him. Overwhelming crowds greeted Him, and it was the state of the people in those anxious masses that grieved Him. Read the passage below to get a glimpse into what Jesus experienced:

> *When he saw the crowds, he had compassion on them, because they were harassed and helpless, like sheep without a shepherd.*
>
> —MATTHEW 9:36

Their lives were a mess. Forces and people they could not manage controlled their lives. They looked like wandering sheep with no leader or caretaker. They had lost their innocence and because of this, Jesus was moved to compassion for them. He loved them, but mourned their condition.

If we could somehow travel back in time to visit with some of these folks, I think we'd find our lives today are not so very different than theirs were two centuries ago. Sure, they didn't have to worry about their kids getting into the "right" schools or the Dow Jones affecting their retirement accounts but, like us, they were concerned with the state of their family, their community, and their country. They also had relentless masters, demanding schedules, and pressures that pushed them to their limits. Same concerns, different details.

Like many of us today, they craved someone who would give them direction and guidance in the midst of what appeared to be a senseless existence. All they knew was all they knew and the hope of anything more was beyond their scope. As a result, they truly were like sheep without a shepherd. More than anything during His ministry on earth, it was people such as these—people such as *us*—that Jesus wanted to touch and transform.

During the last day before His death, Jesus scolded the religious leaders for their hypocrisy and for misguiding their people (Matthew 23:1-36). He then turned His attention to the very people who had been led astray. His heart cried out over their lost condition yet again. He longed for them to know the love He had for them. "O Jerusalem, Jerusalem," Jesus grieved, "you who kill the prophets and stone those sent to you, how often I have longed to gather your children together as a hen gathers her chicks under her wings, but you were not willing" (v. 37). Can't you just imagine the sadness in His voice or sense His genuine mourning over the spiritual condition of those He came to save? He knew His purpose was to live and die for such as these and yet, they couldn't (or wouldn't) accept His identity as the Messiah.

A stellar example of a man who mourned, a good-guy-gone-bad-turned-good-again was King David. As ruler of the nation of Israel, he could (and did!) have an endless supply of women at his beck and call. However it was his attraction to Bathsheba, another man's wife, that put into motion a series of sins that eventually brought the king to his knees in repentance. The regret he felt for his actions is almost palpable in his anguished pleas:

> *For I know my transgressions, and my sin is always before me. Against you, you only, have I sinned and done what is evil in your sight, so that you are proved*

right when you speak and justified when you judge. Surely I was sinful at birth, sinful from the time my mother conceived me.

—PSALM 51:3–5

That's some serious all out, hand-wringing, heartbreaking mourning! Even on my worst days, I probably don't come anywhere near this impassioned confession, but David lived life on a grand scale and so it should come as no surprise his confession followed suit. He knew his spiritual condition had been compromised, he knew it grieved God, and he knew the far-reaching poverty of soul he felt apart from God. We could probably learn a thing or two from his intense brokenness.

Besides confession, mourning over our degenerate and desperate sinful nature can come as a cry of frustration. Paul, in a moment of "Everyman's" anguish, cried out to God over his struggle with sin. "What a wretched man I am! Who will rescue me from this body of death?" (Romans 7:24). Paul confessed he wanted to do what God wanted, but the more he tried, the more he kept doing "the evil I do not want to do" (v. 19). He was fed up, frustrated, and into high-octane mourning over his inability to do what was right.

Who among us hasn't battled this inner demon on issues large and small? You know you shouldn't pass on the latest hearsay about the boss and his assistant, but before you know it, it's all anyone can talk about at the office and the words spill from your mouth like a water wiggle gone wild. Maybe gossip isn't your personal challenge, but

Jesus' promise to those who mourn is comfort.

snagging "one more cookie" (might as well make it an even half dozen) is a temptation you just can't resist. Maybe your incriminations are more personal in nature and you find yourself rationalizing that a little bit of soft porn "won't hurt anyone."

Our personal demons are just that—personal. They lead us where we don't want to go, engage us in otherwise unacceptable behavior, and leave us beating ourselves up when we succumb to them. If left to our own devices, we'll all eventually destroy our lives with sin. It might be sudden and spectacular or subtle and insidious, but either way, unaddressed sin will always eventually lead to a life of frustration and a continual mourning for our depraved condition.

The good news is that Paul was not left to grieve his spiritual condition—and neither are we. God showed Paul a way out and allowed him the glorious revelation as to who would rescue him from his disdainful condition: "Thanks be to God—through Jesus Christ our Lord!" (v. 25). Just like Paul, our earnest and sincere mourning can lead to shouts of joy when we trust Christ to be our salvation from and power over our condition.

The Promise

Jesus' promise to those who mourn is comfort—His comfort—every time we show up, sullied and sinful. The comfort Christ offers in this verse means "to come alongside." For me, this calls to mind the picture of a loving parent coming *alongside* a vulnerable child, offering protection, comfort, and encouragement. The word can also describe an advocate, someone who pleads your case to the judge as he or she stands alongside you. (See 1 John 2:1.)

Jesus not only made a promise to those who mourned, His blessing also revealed *who He was*. Jesus was the comfort He promised to those who grieved their spiritual condition and that of others. Jesus fulfilled God's promise through the prophets that He would send a comforter "to comfort all who mourn" (Isaiah 61:2). And, when Jesus was about to go to His death and ascend to heaven, He promised He would send another "Comforter" to be with His followers forever—the Spirit of truth (John 14:16–17). Jesus promised Himself as the solution to our mournful state of confession and repentance.

As a disciple of Jesus, James echoed much of what Jesus taught to his own followers. James' sentiments reflected a similar promise of comfort for the weary and wandering. In his letter to the Christians of his time, James wrote, "Grieve, mourn and wail. Change your laughter to mourning and your joy to gloom. Humble yourselves before the Lord, and he will lift you up" (James 4:9–11). Then, just as now, humility and sadness were a hard sell to overworked and overstressed men and women. Imagine the vendors in the village square hawking their goods and services on market day. There are fresh-plucked chickens, straight-from-the-vineyard grapes, and crisp and colorful fine linens. And there's one more thing . . . a young man pitching mourning to the masses.

"Ditch your joy; don the sackcloth, sadness for sale!" he yells.

Come again? Abandon the little joy I find in this strife-filled life of goats, camels, and sand storms and replace it with sorrow and rue? Not me, buddy! Find another sucker to take the bait!

And yet, this is just what James was telling the believers of his time to do. He was telling them to see their spiritual condition as God did and not some rationalization of why they did the things they did. He knew if they could get a glimpse of God's holiness they would respond in true repentance and God would respond in kind—through comfort and assurance beyond measure.

The Illness

Up till now we've discussed what mourning looks like and the promise from Christ that accompanies it when true mourning results in repentance and a change in perspective and behavior. But is there a downside to mourning? Can we go too far in carrying the emotional burden of others? Let's be honest . . . not everyone warmly embraces the concept of their own total unworthiness. After all, there are hefty bank accounts, glowing performance reviews, and compelling "you-are-worthy" self-help books that tell us otherwise.

UNHEALTHY MOURNING

Unhealthy mourning can lead to inappropriate forms of depression. Please understand that I am in no way suggesting that depression results *only* from our inability or unwillingness to properly grieve—not the case at all. Life stressors, chemical imbalance, stress, and loss can be major contributors to depression. I do, however, believe that a continued sadness over our sin and the spiritual condition of others without accepting God's offer of forgiveness and comfort can produce a debilitating form of depression.

Consider this: Just as God sees our sins in all their HD/3-D glory, He also sees *past* our dishonoring words, thoughts, and actions to our *potential*. Whether we've taken the step to claim Christ as our Savior or not, God views each of us as potential family members in His heavenly home. Imagine that He's laid out the welcome mat, put a pot of fresh coffee on to brew, and is standing on the front porch anticipating *your* arrival. Who wouldn't want to be welcomed so warmly? And yet so many of us, for a myriad of reasons, resist the invitation to accept Christ's offer. The result is that we can suffer the mental, physical, and emotional consequences of depression brought on from not doing what we *know* to be the right thing.

When taken to an extreme, depression that accompanies our resistance to conviction can have grave consequences. Judas, the one who betrayed Jesus is a prime example. He sinned on an extraordinary level, caved in to his own rationale regarding forgiveness and took his life as a result of it. Read the account of his betrayal-for-hire scheme with the Roman leaders in Matthew 27:1–5. Notice Judas's response when he realized what he had done (vv. 3, 5):

> *When Judas, who had betrayed him, saw that Jesus was condemned, he was seized with remorse and returned the thirty silver coins to the chief priests and the elders.... So Judas threw the money into the temple and left. Then he went away and hanged himself.*

Not exactly an honorable response to the realization of his magnificent sin, is it? It's hard to say what each of us would do given the same circumstances as the oh-so-desperate Judas, but it's not hard to know how Christ would have responded to a repenting and mournful Judas if given the opportunity: forgiveness and acceptance would be my bet. Oh, and no need for that rope, either.

HEALTHY MOURNING

Paul taught, "Godly sorrow brings repentance that leads to salvation and leaves no regret, but worldly sorrow brings death" (2 Corinthians 7:10). He had scolded his friends at Corinth in a previous letter, and he prayed that his rebuff of their offenses would lead to a change in the better in their relationship, *not* more bitterness. Never one to mince words, Paul was as straightforward as he could have been with the Corinthians. He was telling them, in effect, there was no plan B.

I can just see Paul giving a modern-day conference, maybe something along the lines of a Grow Your Faith event to packed-out arenas across the country. There'd be oversized banners hanging from the rafters, vendors selling T-shirts in the foyer, and an excited buzz in the audience. Cue the music. Dim the lights. Live in 3 . . . 2 . . . 1.

"Ladies and gentlemen," the announcer booms.

And then an unassuming man in street clothes takes the stage to thunderous applause. Some people snap pictures with their phones. Others shout cheers of excitement. Even a few air horns blast from the nosebleed section. When at last the audience goes quiet, Paul signals for the first slide.

"GODLY SORROW BRINGS REPENTANCE THAT LEADS TO SALVATION AND LEAVES NO REGRET."

The audience goes wild at the simplicity of Paul's insight. Cue the second slide.

"WORLDLY SORROW BRINGS DEATH."

Again, the audience applauds wildly and then . . . then Paul exits the stage. End of program.

"Thank you for coming," the announcer says, "Please travel safely."

> Confession is the spiritual exercise that allows us to accept the comfort Jesus promises.

What just happened? I'll tell you. Paul, in the most succinct terms possible, summed up Judas's tragic example as a statement of fact of the most basic principle there is regarding faith. Overcome by sorrow for his betrayal, Judas was compelled to take his life—death at his own hands. On the other hand, Paul preached that godly sorrow leads to God's mercy and *away* from self-condemnation. Godly sorrow and mourning lead to salvation and forgiveness for all.

It's important to note here that, while Jesus wants each of us to arrive at this state of mourning in order to receive His comfort and blessings, He does not want us to *stay* bereaved and overcome by our sinful tendencies. He wants us to change and go forward as shining examples of His power.

The Exercise

Remember Dave from the previous chapter and how he grew to realize just how poor in spirit he truly was? He overcame his remorse over his sin by confessing first to his wife, then to his accountability partners, then to me. Confession is admitting your sin to significant others. And for Dave, confession was also a key part of enabling him to move from mourning his sin to overcoming his sin.

His godly sorrow led to repentance and hope for the future, but it wasn't something he accomplished on his own. His accountability partners proactively put a Web blocker on his computers to prevent Dave from getting to the Web sites that drew him into sin—and they kept the passwords! These guys loved Dave enough to do something to help him after he confessed his sin to them. This kind of help shows the positive power a community of like-minded believers can have on struggling individuals.

Confession is the spiritual exercise that allows us to accept the comfort Jesus promises. Scripture promises that forgiveness follows confession (1 John 1:9) and *community* is the context in which confession is best practiced. Community keeps confession within healthy relationships and provides the accountability needed to move beyond the sin to a life that honors God.

James was adamant about the need to confess our sins to one another and to pray for each other. It wasn't a suggested activity as far as he was concerned; it was a directive:

> *Confess your sins to each other and pray for each other so that you may be healed. The prayer of a righteous man is powerful and effective.*
>
> —JAMES 5:16

When we understand that *confession* literally means "to say the same thing," we realize that to confess simply means we are agreeing with God about the way things *are*. Not how we *should* have acted. Or how we had *planned* to respond. Or even how we had *prayed* we would reply. But, *how things are* as a result of our words and actions and thoughts.

It's also important to realize that when we confess, we're not telling God something that He doesn't already know. Recall how He's got that omniscience thing working for Him? God already knows it all. Confession is for *us*. It allows us the opportunity to accept His assessment for our misdeeds as well as receive His forgiveness when we open our hearts to His grace.

Many of us are reluctant to engage in such transparency.

One of today's most insightful Christian authors, John Ortberg, offers this explanation of why we confess, "Confession is not primarily something God has us do because he needs it. God is not clutching tightly to his mercy, as if we had to pry it from his fingers like a child's last cookie. We need to confess in order to heal and be changed."[1] This same explanation applies when we confess our sins to others committed to helping us maintain our spiritual well-being.

When Dave confessed his sin to his wife, he was not telling her something she did not already know. She had caught him! His confession told her how he felt and how he knew he had hurt her. And while he volunteered his lapse to his accountability buddies, he didn't have to tell them that looking at inappropriate pictures online was wrong. They had agreed on that and had committed to helping Dave steer clear of his temptation. When he came to his friends, he was agreeing with his Christian brothers that he had wronged them by breaking their trust and that he had wronged God by acting inappropriately. He was sending up an SOS that read, "Come quick! I need you!"

If we're fortunate enough to have access to a group similar to Dave's, we also can experience support, solutions, and compassion. *When confession is exercised in a community, our hearts are better prepared to receive God's forgiveness and mercy.* However, many of us are reluctant to engage in such transparency. This is due, in large part, to our tendency to see our mistakes as so much more indicting in comparison to the shortcomings of others.

Pastor Peter Scazzero describes an emotionally healthy church—people gathered in community for worship and service to God—

> [as people who] . . . take a deep, hard look inside their hearts, asking, "What is going on that Jesus Christ is trying to change? They understand that a person's life is like an iceberg, with the vast majority of who we are lying deep beneath the surface. They invite God to bring to their awareness and to transform those beneath-the-surface layers that hinder them from becoming more like Jesus Christ.[2]

Wow! That hits more than just a little too close to home for my comfort. However, it helps to remember it was God's design for us to experience His forgiveness with others who also have been forgiven, those who have been willing to look below the surface of their public lives in order to expose their hearts to the community of faith. This way we are not alone in our sin, which leads to unhealthy mourning. When we are renewed in community we are also prevented from becoming proud of our personal piety. Confession in community is God's plan to help us achieve and maintain spiritual wellness. It is the door to God's forgiveness that begins in sorrow, but leads to joy.

Takeaway

This step on our journey of spiritual health is godly sorrow that leads to repentance and the comfort of God's forgiveness. From the valley of spiritual poverty God draws us one step closer to the summit of an encounter with Him. Our healthy response to our true spiritual condition leads to joyful forgiveness and authentic community with others, but God does not want us to stay there. The next stop on our journey is meekness that grows out of humbling ourselves to confess our sin to God and others.

Questions for Reflection

1. What was your first emotion when you read this beatitude?

2. When was a time you mourned and were comforted by a friend or by God?

3. Tell of a time when mourning led to depression or an unhealthy expression of your sadness? How did you recover from that emotional/spiritual state?

4. Describe a time when you mourned your spiritual condition or that of others. What did you do in response to that sense of mourning?

5. How do you practice the exercise of confession in community with others? If you do not, what are some reasons this is hard for you?

CHAPTER 5

The Meek

Blessed are the meek, for they will inherit the earth.

—Matthew 5:5

My friend Ron is a former professional athlete who had a long history of being overly aggressive. Rock-hard muscles, amped-up adrenaline, and a healthy dose of testosterone were the primary driving forces of his younger years. In fact, it wasn't unusual for Ron to rely on all three of these influences if ever he found himself at odds with someone. His friends used to joke that Ron would walk a mile just to have a good fight. Brawn triumphed over brain every time for him.

I hadn't seen Ron in a few years and had no reason to suspect much had changed as far as his preferred method of resolving conflicts. So when he stopped by my office one day to visit and we headed out to lunch together, I watched with curiosity as he navigated an overcrowded parking lot full of holiday shoppers. After circling the lot a few times, we finally spotted a parking space two rows over. We soon realized we weren't the only ones who had seen the open space when a pickup truck going the wrong way barreled up the row and made a cock-eyed swing into the spot.

Now, there was *no* way that truck was going to fit into that spot—we knew it, they knew it, and they knew *we* knew it—but that didn't stop these two good ol' boys from putting it in park until we conceded and moved on. That's when things got *really* strange.

The "old" Ron would have jumped at the chance to settle this game of parking lot chicken by hosting his own version of a holiday smackdown right there on the asphalt.

"Mess with me, buddy?"

"Not today, you're not."

However, what I quickly came to realize was that the "old" Ron was gone. Anger, aggression, and violence were no longer his personal default setting. Instead, in what could only be described as a moment of grown-up maturity, Ron flashed the men a genuine smile and a hearty wave and drove on.

Was it weakness on Ron's part not to challenge the guys for the parking spot?

Did he fear being outnumbered?

Had the holiday spirit taken hold of him to the point that he really was showing goodwill toward all men?

No. No. And no.

The "new" Ron had received Christ, embraced His teachings, and was a living, breathing testament to the power of meekness.

The People

If I asked you to describe someone who is emotionally healthy, what characteristics would you choose?

Realistic, yet confident of their abilities?

Balanced with regards to the stressors in their life?

Maybe even insightful in terms of accepting what they can't control?

It was this other-centeredness that set the meek apart.

What about describing someone who is physically healthy?

Well-developed muscle tone?

Cardio stamina?

Acceptable readings on their cholesterol, blood pressure, or blood sugar levels?

It's relatively easy for most of us to identify quickly at least a few characteristics of what we consider healthy in terms of our bodies and our minds. But, ask people to identify what makes a person healthy spiritually, and you'll get all sorts of vague and random answers.

Honest? Sounds good.

Honorable? That always helps.

Prayerful? Naturally. You can't be spiritual without being prayerful, right?

All of those are suitable answers, but there's one tremendously important trait that very rarely makes the list when describing the spiritually fit: *meek.*

Meek?

You read it right. *Meek.*

Not weak.

Not meager.

Not even mellow.

Meek . . . as in those *who* will inherit the earth.

Jesus identified the meek in His sermon that day on the hillside: those who were gentle, unassertive, and humble toward others. In fact, on that day in particular, they were probably the ones easy to spot in the back row as hundreds of others pushed and pulled their way through the crowd trying to hear and see Jesus better.

It was this other-centeredness that set the meek apart from the rest of the crowd and, because of this, Jesus blessed them as kingdom people. He wanted them to know that their apparent weakness as humble and meek people could actually form the basis of an eternal relationship with Him. Never mind that others saw them as weak; He saw them as willing to submit their will to a higher purpose or authority.

Probably the best example of this willingness to submit to a higher authority is illustrated in the military where rank determines the hierarchy of responsibility. The sergeant tells

the private to jump; the private asks, "How high?" The major tells the sergeant to jump; the sergeant asks, "How high?" And so on. This was clearly the case during the time of Roman rule as the centurion in Matthew 8:5–10 illustrated:

> *When Jesus had entered Capernaum, a centurion came to him, asking for help. "Lord," he said, "my servant lies at home paralyzed and in terrible suffering."*
>
> *Jesus said to him, "I will go and heal him."*
>
> *The centurion replied, "Lord, I do not deserve to have you come under my roof. But just say the word, and my servant will be healed. For I myself am a man under authority, with soldiers under me. I tell this one, 'Go,' and he goes; and that one, 'Come,' and he comes. I say to my servant, 'Do this,' and he does it."*

> *When Jesus heard this, he was astonished and said to those following him, "I tell you the truth, I have not found anyone in Israel with such great faith."*

The centurion, a man of power and rank in the Roman army, exhibited great faith and meekness because he understood authority. He applied what life as a soldier had taught him about authority to his relationship with Jesus. In return, he received the praises of Jesus.

Jesus looked for people who would give their lives to Him so He could work powerfully in them. He realized that people accustomed to submitting to a superior were stellar candidates for serving Him wholeheartedly. He challenged His followers to choose *meek* over *mighty* as a reflection of their love for Him.

The Characteristic

You know those dramatic makeovers they show on many of the daytime talk shows? The ones where the producers select the homeliest, most unkempt member of the studio audience (usually a frumpy, stuck-in-the-1980s-looking woman) and whisk her backstage for a head-to-toe redo while the show is taping. When they finally reveal the coiffed-up, dressed-up, jazzed-up model, more often than not, she looks nothing (and I mean absolutely *nothing!*) like the person she was an hour earlier. I share this analogy because that's what has happened to *meek* in the last 2,000 years; the character trait resembles nothing like what it was originally intended to mean.

In Jesus' day, the word *meek* meant "power under control." It also meant "gentle." Greek philosophers considered persons meek whose character showed neither fury nor righteous anger.

People were viewed as meek when they were polite, kind toward others, and showed self-restraint. But being meek wasn't just limited to interactions with other people; it was also viewed as the core of who you were becoming in Christ Jesus.

Jesus modeled meekness as He brought the power and resources of His life under the will of His Father. He had submitted His life to God's plan. When Jesus spoke of the meek, He did not mean those who had good manners and who were humble by nature. He was referring to a supernatural meekness that came about as a result of a personal relationship with God and subsequent submission to God's plan for one's life.

Meekness is also listed as one of the fruits of the Spirit (Galatians 5:22–23), which means it is a gift from the Holy Spirit. This gift becomes evident when the Spirit is within our lives. All of the fruits of the Spirit become increasingly more a part of our character as we give our lives to Christ. The more we become like Jesus, the more these are reflected in our behavior, attitudes, and relationships. Each one of the fruits of the Spirit are excellent benchmarks for spiritual wellness.

The Apostle Paul had a unique perspective of a new life in Christ: he likened it to a new wardrobe that we wear in place of our old one (Colossians 3:12). Gentleness or meekness was to be one of those pieces of new clothing. The implication is that others should notice our meek behavior as they would a new sweater or dress. While we don't wear these new items to show them off or flaunt them, we wear them to demonstrate a new taste in how we live our lives. And unlike the newest fashions, the hottest colors, or the changing seasons, this is one item of "clothing" that doesn't change with the culture.

Meekness is evidence that the Spirit of God lives in us. It is what we clothe ourselves with as we put on our new life in Christ. As we live out the life to which God has called each of us in Christ, we are to live as Jesus did—in gentleness and meekness. A characteristic of being a follower of Jesus and being spiritually well is that we consistently exhibit meekness in our lives. If it's not regularly present, then chances are we haven't become fully convicted of the poverty of our soul and mourned our sin. If these traits are fully embraced, meekness is a natural progression.

The Promise

I see the promise that the meek shall inherit the earth fulfilled in two ways. Simply stated, unless we are submitted to God's control we will be controlled by our possessions and the opinions of others. This is a universal spiritual principle.

Think you're an exception? Ask yourself the following:

"Do I ever allow the balances on my bank and credit card accounts to determine my mood for a day or a week or longer?" Maybe you've done the math and figured out that if you live to be 145, you'll be completely out of debt. Otherwise, your children's inheritance will consist of little more than a hefty stack of IOUs and Grandma's china cabinet.

"Do I think my life would be just perfect *if only* I had this car/ that big screen/a beautiful new home?" Say your neighbor pulls into his driveway with a brand-new, odometer-still-in-the-double-digits car. Ouch! Makes your beater with the coat hanger antenna and the custom crayon artwork on the console look a bit pathetic in comparison.

And lastly, consider asking yourself, "Do I always define the good life as a destination, an end goal, of my life?" Sure, you think *my life sucks now*, but *someday* . . . when the kids are grown, when you're retired or when you're free to travel the world . . . *then* life will be enjoyable and fulfilling. But until *then*, this grind you call your life is just a means to an end, a way to make tomorrow happen, and a necessary evil.

If you answered yes to any (or all!) of these, welcome to the human condition. You're not alone. Quite the contrary; you're in the company of just about *everyone* who has made it past their 20th birthday. It's a *natural* state, but it doesn't have to be a *permanent* state. In fact, those of us who move past this dependence on worldly possessions and on to total dependence on Christ are the very ones Jesus is addressing when He claims "the meek will . . . inherit the earth" (Matthew 5:4). The meek are truly the only ones who *can* inherit the earth because everyone else is held captive to the very things they are trying to capture.

The promise of this verse has a second, and profoundly more biblical, fulfillment. Jesus promised His first hearers that they would inherit the earth. In this instance, earth can be translated to mean *land*, as in "the promised land." The Jewish people who heard Jesus most certainly made this connection. They knew that when God called Abraham from his homeland, He told him to take the land "from the river of Egypt to the great river, the Euphrates" (Genesis 15:18). When Jesus first said the meek would inherit the earth, the crowd heard Him promise the land that God had promised them through their father Abraham.

> It was as if He said, "Happy are you if you are beat down."

So Jesus said *the promised land would belong* to those who were among the least likely candidates living during Jesus' time on earth. It's completely understandable that their collective ears perked up when they heard this exciting promise—especially in a land occupied by the Roman army at the time. Jesus turned the tables of power upside down when He made this declaration about those who would inherit His kingdom. It would be like the worst one on the Little League team getting picked to play for the Yankees. Or the small-time investor buying Google when it was $3 a share. Or, even like the unknown author waking up to find his book on the *New York Times* best-seller list. This promise was seemingly impossible, outlandish, unbelievable, even unfathomable; it was all these things and more—it was *true*.

The promise was payback—unmerited, unexpected, and wildly rewarding to those who accepted and honored Christ's contrarian words. It was as if He said, "Happy are you if you are beat down, if you are afraid to decide, if you are pushed out of line in the marketplace. *You* will inherit the land promised to your fathers, because you can give your life wholly to God, so God can give you what He desires for you."

Romans 8:17 provides vital information about who we are in Christ: "Now if we are children, then we are heirs—heirs of God and co-heirs with Christ, if indeed we share in his sufferings in order that we may also share in his glory." In this verse, Paul identified our standing with God. I like to illustrate it like this: just when you realize that you are trapped hopelessly in sin, God comes and adopts you. He pays the price of adoption with the sacrifice of His only Son. The payment frees you from slavery to sin. You find that you have become God's child. Now that you are a child of God, He informs you that your new position makes you His heir and co-heir with Jesus Christ.[1]

A counterfeit form of meekness can lead to passivity.

The land was physical evidence of God's covenant with His people. To possess the land was to receive the promise of God's covenant, but the promise of God's inheritance shifted from possession of the land of the old covenant to a relationship with God through Jesus, which was the New Covenant (1 Corinthians 11:25). This astounding promise of inheriting the land as part of the New Covenant carries with it many benefits—membership in the family of God, status as an heir of God, and a place in His eternal kingdom, *and* it applies to each person who chooses to follow Him.

The Illness

When meekness is out of balance, the results can become spiritual and emotional illnesses. Remember that authentic meekness does not mean weakness. It means a life willingly surrendered to God's control. However, *a counterfeit form of meekness can lead to passivity, loss of boundaries, and even self-destructiveness. Codependency* is the buzzword pop culture frequently uses to describe the loss of personal identity. That results in allowing others to make our decisions or our being unable to put limits on others' behavior as they relate to our lives.

Some behaviors that may look like traits of meekness are actually signs of spiritual illness. When we blindly allow others to lead us, authentic meekness is *not* the result. Feelings of worthlessness and loss of hope frequently become part of our lives. Codependency means a loss of personal identity in which we feel that we must serve, help, or fix others and that we have no choice in the matter. In codependent mode our identity depends on what those other people think of us. Genuine meekness begins with a *willing* submission to God that can only come from a healthy identity in Christ.

Ironically, counterfeit meekness has an even darker side than codependency. *Those who perceive themselves to be weak may overcompensate with power plays over others.* Seeing their own weakness, they may act aggressively toward others to overcome their sense of powerlessness. This is often the case in instances of abuse. As demeaned and demoralized as victims feel at the hands of their abuser, they frequently repeat the cycle as a means of establishing *their* power over someone else. The helplessness and victimization of abuse leaves the abused feeling weak *and* meek. As a result, they often try to overcome these misplaced emotions by inflicting unnecessary power or control over others. Sadly, it is those who fear meekness and perceive it as a sign of weakness who most frequently refuse to surrender their lives to God for fear of losing control of their situation. In fact, just the opposite is true; by surrendering the issues of our lives to Christ we're given supreme control because we've placed whatever problems, challenges, and conflicts we have into His fully capable, all-powerful, caring hands.

Another indication of meekness taken to an extreme is cynicism. When we allow hurtful circumstances to produce a critical outlook on our lives, on others, and on God, we become cynical.

"No reason to hope for a better today because yesterday was such a downer."

"Why get involved with those friends when it always leads to disappointment anyway?"

"And God? Yeah, well, best I can tell, He hasn't exactly delivered on those prayers I keep sending His way. I mean, really, why bother with little more than getting through the day? The way I see it, life's a drag . . . and then you die."

Cynical people can discount just about every sentiment you send their way. The glass-half-empty perspective has a way of becoming a self-fulfilling prophecy: you think the worst is going to happen and (surprise!) it does! When a cynic begins to embrace a healthy perspective of being meek, it's a supernatural occurrence of the first degree. No amount of cajoling, no woulda/coulda/shouldas, no *nothing* can convince some people of Christ's true intent in being meek. However, when He steps in, the changes can be a complete about face.

Harvard professors and authors Ronald Heifetz and Marty

Linsky warn leaders against losing heart and allowing innocence to turn into cynicism that is dressed up as realism. They warn:

> The cynical brand of realism, which assumes the worst will happen, is a way of protecting yourself by lowering your aspirations so that you will never be disappointed. It's like an insurance policy. If things go well, boy, that's terrific. But if you never expect anything to work out, you're never surprised, and, more to the point, you never have to experience frustration.[2]

This particular "cloak of self-protection to insulate themselves from the dangers of stepping out" suffocates the very "aliveness we strive to protect."

Finally, *false meekness can lead to judgmental behavior.* We tell ourselves that we're not as bad as they are. We position ourselves above our inner circle and question the motives and morality of those outside our immediate circle of influence. When we seek to build ourselves up by tearing others down, we develop judgmental attitudes that build barriers between otherwise well-meaning people. It's a tragic end result when we allow puffed up perspectives of ourselves to become the tear in the fabric of friendship.

The Exercise

When I consider what we each can do to allow the practice of the meekness of Christ to become more relevant in our lives, two exercises immediately come to mind. Be warned, however, like saying, "Oh, I will remove processed sugar and grains from my diet," these two simple concepts can be terribly challenging to integrate fully into our lives. The two spiritual disciplines that help further our complete understanding of meekness are *submission* and *accountability.*

We live in a culture that exalts individualism and encourages us to bow to no one. This counterculture move to meekness is, perhaps, one the most difficult to adopt sincerely. We know that "the common quality is, rather, the state of powerlessness: inability to forward one's own cause; and in every case God either is, does, will, may be expected to, or should come to the rescue."[3] Our culture does not honor or encourage any of those realities. And, God coming to the rescue is completely outside our do-it-yourself worldview. Indeed, few people want to hear talk of submitting to another individual or becoming accountable. But, what is submission?

SUBMISSION

Submission is the *S* word to some. It is not a concept we embrace in a free society. I observed elsewhere:

> We resist submission to another person with every fiber of our cholesterol-free lifestyles. In a culture where the individual has reached godlike status, submitting to anyone or anything outside ourselves is beyond reason. Self interest soars high above service in our hierarchy of interests. These attitudes . . . are also the very feelings that prevent us from knowing the freedom that comes from giving ourselves to Christ.[4]

As a spiritual exercise, this behavior is like submitting yourself to another to learn a skill. For example, to learn to play the piano you submit yourself to a teacher who drills you and gives you exercises to play between lessons. If you want to learn to play the piano, you will do what the teacher says. Virtuosos are not self-made! Even great performers have teachers who guide them. They are apprentices before they are masters of their skill. It is unfortunate that we as Christians have forgotten this truth.

This is true in just about every learned skill we engage in every day. For example, consider cooking. Whether your training is formal in nature (think home economics class or culinary arts courses) or less structured (watching Grandma bake her famous triple chocolate cake from scratch), no one ever really wakes up one morning and whips out a flawless four-course meal without a bit of instruction somewhere in their past.

The same is true in all levels of sports too. From City League football to the NFL, players are educated, encouraged, and shaped by coaches at all levels. Because coaches have the perspective of observing their players in practice and on game day, they can readily identify strengths, weaknesses, and areas requiring improvement. It is the wise football player that heeds the instruction, makes the corrections, and puts into practice the direction of his coach. After all, by controlling a player's time on the field, the coach ultimately controls a player's effectiveness and longevity in the sport. Take away the shoulder pads, the helmets, and the *x*'s and *o*'s and replace the coach with Christ. Kind of resembles the way we are to live as Christ followers, doesn't it? Like a coach, Christ observes us in the practice of daily life as well as our own personal game days, times we are put to the test. He sees the areas we need to improve, provides instruction through His Word, and allows circumstances to prevail in our lives that provide the opportunity for us to demonstrate our mastery of His lessons. And finally, just as the coach wants his players to represent their team to the best of their abilities, Christ also wants His followers to bring their A game to their workplace, their school, their home—wherever they meet opposition and obstacles in a fallen world.

Through this practice of submission to Christ we engage in self-denial of our rights as rulers of our lives and submit to God's rule. This is a daily habit for those who would become like Jesus. Just as concert pianists give up their right to play a piece however they want and submit their talents to the desires of the composer and the directions of the teacher, so followers of Jesus give up their rights to live however they feel and choose to do as the Master leads. Please note, however, that there is a significant difference between self-denial and self-neglect. Caring for our bodies properly is a form of submission.

As I understand the Beatitudes, submission is the beginning of meekness. To submit myself to God and to the spiritual direction of a more mature Christian is to allow the spiritual characteristics of meekness to grow in my life. But how do we actually *learn* to practice submission?

1. Begin by confessing to God your pride. Pride prevents the development of meekness. Pride is the rival god that causes us to sin. Self-centeredness prevents us from submitting to God's leadership. Poverty of soul and grieving over our spiritual condition can lead us to the place of submission. Our confession can simply be, "*God, I am helpless without You. I give You control of my life. Tame me with Your Spirit and Word. Mold me into the person You desire me to become.*"

2. Submit to the lordship of Jesus on a daily basis. "Jesus is Lord" is the simplest and plainest confession of faith (Romans 10:9). This daily confession, followed by intentional decisions to allow God to lead our actions, will make room in our hearts for the characteristic of meekness to grow. Self-denial is simply placing God's agenda before our own and obediently following it.

3. Make yourself accountable to a small group of Jesus' followers. Like a new piano student finding a master teacher, we need a small group of disciples who will keep us true to our commitments to Christ.

Accountability is a risk of trust.

ACCOUNTABILITY

In order to work toward spiritual meekness, we all have to have the ability to account for who we are (not just who we *profess* to be), what we have done, and what we are currently engaged in. By maintaining accountability with other believers, we are encouraged (sometimes subtly, sometimes directly) to nurture the meekness in our lives.

I must admit that this spiritual practice is as hard for me as giving up ice cream for fruit. The reason is that accountability is based on trust, and trust is built over years but can be broken in a moment. In order for me to be accountable to you, I must trust you with my secrets and my dreams. If you have been around as long as I have, you will have many stories of people you have trusted with your stuff but soon discovered others knew about it too. My cautious side lives by the adage attributed to Benjamin Franklin, "The only way to keep a secret between three people is if two of them are dead." Accountability is a risk of trust. But we know that all healthy relationships are built upon the fragile foundation of trust held in the hands of imperfect people.

I have discovered and had the privilege of witnessing men and women dramatically change their behavior through authentic accountability to a small group of Christians who have committed to follow Jesus with all of their heart, mind, strength, and soul. It's not necessarily an easy task, but it is certainly doable. What oftentimes starts out as an awkward exchange of surface-level prayer requests can have the potential to develop into a sacred discipline among those committed to each other. I've seen it happen many, many times, but it requires the discipline of regularly giving another person who loves you the right to examine any and every part of your life to help you become more like Jesus. As relationships within the group strengthen, so also does trust. When trust is in place, transparency among members soon follows and that is where the *real* growth in spiritual maturity takes place. It's a process, not a one-time event. It's a journey, not a destination.

Takeaway

We've addressed the first three steps on the journey to spiritual wellness. Poverty of soul leads to repentant mourning over our spiritual condition. Repentance leads us to give all of our lives to God for His purposes. Meekness is the by-product of obedient submission to God. Jesus blessed those who are meek and promised them they would be free from the control of earthly possessions and would inherit the promised things of God. We're approaching the summit of our trek on our journey to better understanding these life-altering, life-guiding words of Christ called the Beatitudes. Our next stop will show us the satisfaction that awaits us in a full and meaningful relationship with God as we see how our deepening relationship with Him leads to hungering and thirsting for more.

Questions for Reflection

1. Write your first impression of meekness when you began this chapter. How has that changed after reading this chapter?

2. In what areas of your life have you submitted your wishes to someone else? List the activity and the person's name.

3. In what areas of your life have you submitted your wishes to Christ? List the activity and how Christ has led you in that activity.

4. To whom are you accountable for your personal and spiritual life? How has that person helped you in your relationship with God?

CHAPTER 6

Those Who Hunger and Thirst

Blessed are those who hunger and thirst for righteousness, for they will be filled.

—Matthew 5:6

Up to this point, the first three characteristics Jesus blessed pointed us to a closer relationship with God. When we become *poor in spirit*, we experience a realization of our emptiness; this leads us to *mourn* our spiritual condition as we become more and more aware of our guilt and our helpless and hopeless situation apart from God. *Meekness* soon follows as we abandon all sense of personal control and submit to Christ. This move from poverty of soul to mournful state to meekness of spirit is a spiritually seismic shift—from depending on self to dependence on God. The result of our increased dependence on God is a spiritual *hunger and thirst for righteousness.*

Regardless of where we begin and what emotional baggage we bring into our relationship with Christ, the steps we each take on our respective paths to spiritual maturity all have similar benchmarks. To be sure, your background is different from mine, and though we each have a different Christ-appointed journey in receiving and accepting Christ, we all will experience similar realizations, concessions, and confessions as we grow in Christ. It's kind of like saying *your aha* moment may come much earlier in your walk with Christ than *mine*, but timing isn't the issue—arriving at the moment is.

You have to address your survival before you can begin helping others survive.

Let's get back to the mountain-climbing analogy. Climbing to the summit of a mountaintop, Mount Rainier at 14,410 feet, for example, requires climbers to expend considerable physical resources. We burn energy. We get hungry. We dehydrate through perspiration even in the cold. We get thirsty. By the time we reach the top, we're spent and in need of replenishing—and we are only halfway on our journey. We have to get down!

Climbing the summit of God's mighty presence is a journey that begins by exposing our tremendous lack of personal resources. And like on a physical climb, when our resources run out, we begin to hunger and thirst. The difference is that in tackling a mountain of spiritual growth, what we hunger and thirst for is refreshment that only God can give our craving souls.

The progression of spiritual growth for most of us looks something like this:

> Conviction of sin → repentance → submission to God's leadership → desire for God and the things of God

Through this transformation, God prepares you to reenter your relationship with others in ways that will bring His love to them. It's not unlike the concept behind the preflight routine that flight attendants share with passengers regarding the safety precautions and emergency air masks. Without exception, passengers are always instructed to secure their own mask before assisting others. It's the same for spiritual growth: you have to address your survival before you can begin helping others survive. This movement through the Beatitudes ultimately leads us away from our natural self-centeredness once we're securely on the proper path to better knowing God personally. The lifestyle disciplines we develop throughout this journey develop strong and sturdy roots when we practice feeding ourselves with God's righteousness.

Charles Swindoll captured Jesus' intent of this verse with this explanation:

> This beatitude reflects true spiritual passion, an insatiable hunger to know God intimately, to model His ways personally. Don't misread this. Jesus is not talking about merely increasing one's knowledge of biblical truth or doctrinal facts, though there is certainly nothing wrong with either. Instead, He's talking about aligning oneself with God's character: holiness, truth, goodness, and righteousness. . . . Best of all, as with physical hunger and thirst, this spiritual appetite is an ongoing desire, needing to be replenished on a daily basis.[1]

Our journey with Jesus from the valley of our relationships to the mountaintop of His presence produces a spiritual hunger and thirst for Him that He alone can satisfy. But, that He does with abundance.

When Jesus was speaking of those who "hunger and thirst for righteousness," He wasn't referring to those who *already* possessed righteousness, but rather all of His followers, past and present, who *desired* righteousness. He was searching for those who wanted to become Christlike, or righteous, as much as they wanted their next meal or next drink. Just as our body uses the signals of hunger and thirst to keep us alive by reminding us to eat and drink, our spiritual bodies, our souls, also have hunger and thirst signals of a different sort to remind us to replenish those distinct needs too. Your stomach might not growl and your mouth won't become parched, but your soul has its own unique signals that trigger the need for restoration. Sadly, many of us hit the snooze button on our spiritual alarm clocks

and try to meet this longing with other unsuitable options.

Some of us ignore the emptiness with an afternoon at the mall and a new pair of shoes. Others look for fulfillment in our monthly billings to clients. Still others choke down a couple of chili cheeseburgers and a tub of ice cream in the loneliness of the evening. We run into problems when we try to satisfy our spirit's hunger for God with other things. Not only are these short-lived solutions a means to a fleeting end, but they also ignore the greater, deeper spiritual need Christ put in place when we accepted Him. When we experience genuine Christ-created spiritual hunger and thirst, no earthly solution can fill what it is we desire and that is satisfaction in a relationship with God.

Jesus blessed those who were hungry and thirsty for righteousness, those who knew right from wrong, and those who were frustrated because others didn't. They may have longed to be right with God, but because their sins were so vivid, they could not be satisfied until God forgave them and declared them right in His eyes. They came to Jesus expectantly, hoping to find forgiveness. They may have meekly turned to God and longed to be satisfied by His presence. They had tried everything else to fill the hole in their souls, but they were empty and without a sense of right direction in their lives. Nothing else satisfied their souls, so they sought out Jesus.

Jesus blessed those who hunger and for thirst for righteousness because they desired to know God. Their spiritual condition had created an emptiness that drove them to seek out God as the food and water of their souls. Jesus congratulated these people because they were ready to be filled by God's presence.

Jesus blesses us when we seek to find our spiritual nourishment in Him. He congratulates us when we stop filling the emptiness of our soul with unhealthy substitutes. Jesus is saying to us, *"Happy are you when you hunger and thirst after Me for you will be satisfied indeed!"*

The Characteristic

Righteousness means *to be put right with or the act of doing what God requires, doing what is right.*[2] When you speak of righteousness, it has several meanings. It can describe a characteristic of God, our desired standing before Him, or our actions toward others.

RIGHTEOUSNESS AS A CHARACTERISTIC OF GOD

The Book of Psalms sings of God's righteousness in several instances:

> *"Like your name, O God, your praise reaches to the ends of the earth; your right hand is filled with righteousness" (Psalm 48:10).*
>
> *"And the heavens proclaim his righteousness, for God himself is judge" (Psalm 50:6).*
>
> *"Your righteousness reaches to the skies, O God, you who have done great things. Who, O God, is like you?" (Psalm 71:19).*

To hunger and thirst for righteousness is to hunger and thirst for God. Jesus blessed those who desired the character of God.

RIGHTEOUSNESS AS OUR STANDING BEFORE GOD

Righteousness is also our desired spiritual condition before God. To be right before Holy God is to know peace and to have the security of eternal life (Romans 5:1–2). Jesus introduced a new righteousness as He introduced His kingdom. He redefined an old covenant concept to His followers.

Again, Swindoll provides an explanation of what he sees as the practical perspective of this fourth beatitude:

> It includes not just looking upward, pursuing a vertical holiness, but also looking around and being grieved over the corruption, the inequities, the gross lack of integrity, the moral compromises that abound. The servant "hungers and thirsts" for right on earth. Unwilling simply to sigh and shrug off the lack of justice and

> purity as inevitable, servants press on for righteousness. Some would call them idealists or dreamers.[3]

Notice the present-tense verb he uses there. Striving for righteousness is not something people did back in Bible days or people do in war-torn countries with evil regimes. To press on for righteousness is an ongoing experience and a day-to-day event just as viable to twenty-first-century believers as it was during Jesus' time. Ours is not the first generation to wonder what our role is regarding pursuing righteousness.

For those who heard Jesus that day, righteousness was accomplished one line item after another. Complete them all and congratulations, you've arrived at "destination righteous." The problem with their interpretation was that it was in direct opposition to the intention of Jesus' teachings. As Jesus explained it, not only was righteousness not a matter of completing steps one, two, and three; it was something no one individual could accomplish on his own because no one is sufficient in his own glory to stand before God. To be righteous in Jesus' kingdom, you need a different way of being right with God. Jesus revealed the truth that He was the one and only way to God (John 14:6) and that a person becomes righteous in God's eyes only through a relationship with Jesus (2 Corinthians 5:21).

The Word of God reiterates that we become righteous before God in only one way: we must receive the righteousness of God "through faith in Jesus Christ to all who believe" (Romans 3:22). You become righteous before Holy God through trusting that Jesus took your sins upon the cross and covered them with His blood. It was God's plan to have His Son become as sin so that each of us could become righteous in His sight.

RIGHTEOUSNESS CONCERNING OUR ACTIONS BEFORE OTHERS

Rightness before Holy God leads to a new way of living before others. Jesus taught His followers how to live as righteous people. He singled out the Pharisees and Sadducees as prime examples of those who could *look* and *act* righteous, but not truly *be* righteous (Matthew 23). He despised hypocrisy and called His people to a secret piety in which God looks upon our heart to know our motives—the *real* reason why we act the way we do.

If what you do, how you do it, and why you do it is because of your strong desire for a right relationship with God and others, you will become like a starving man. All that you do and say and think will be focused upon satisfying that hunger through an authentic relationship with Christ. The blessings that follow will fill you beyond your wildest dreams.

The Promise

Jesus promised that those who hunger and thirst after righteousness will be satisfied. It was the very reason He came to earth—to fill the emptiness in our souls and to satisfy our deepest longings. The word *satisfied* means to be filled continually as at a banquet table or family feast. That makes me think of Thanksgiving at our house. This is when all the family cooks come together to make, bake, and mash their personal bests in the kitchen. We gather around the table(s) in a big circle with those who could travel to make the day, and someone reads Psalm 100 from the family Bible. I remember the first time my father asked me to read for the family. I felt I had found my place among the spiritual leaders of my clan. I also remember the year I asked my oldest daughter to read for the family. That was a special day of blessing for her and a way to pass on a spiritual tradition to her family. Once we have shared what we were thankful for that year, we stuff ourselves sinfully, sit back and are thankful we are filled up! And you know what? I love *every* moment of it! Not another day of the year *satisfies* me like Turkey Day.

But food alone does not give you a feeling of fullness. When I have a good workout, I feel satisfied. Finishing a weight circuit or laps in the pool, I am satisfied physically. After I have sat with Kim, my wife, and watched an episode of our favorite television series, I am satisfied emotionally. When I have spent time with my grandchildren, although I am tired and I still have to put up tricycles and toys, I am filled with the fullness of being a grandparent. When I leave coffee and conversation with a friend and we have talked about everything from his soul to our plans to climb a 14er together, I am filled with the reality of friendship. Fullness comes in all kinds of packages. The Bible speaks of fullness too.

When Matthew recorded how the 5,000 felt after they had eaten what Jesus blessed and passed out to them via the disciples, he wrote, "And they all ate and were satisfied" (Matthew 14:20). This word for *satisfied* is the same one Jesus used in this beatitude. In Paul's famous declaration, he declared he had learned to be content when he was "well fed"; the same word Jesus used to describe those who would

> Obesity, anorexia, and bulimia stem from improperly satisfying our natural, God-given hunger and thirst for food and water.

sit at His table of righteousness (Philippians 4:12). Paul also announced he had learned to be content in poverty, wealth, and hunger. This mysterious condition came from his unwavering confidence that he could do "all things through him" who gave him strength. The writer of the Psalms sang: I will praise you as long as I live, and in your name I will lift up my hands. *My soul will be satisfied as with the richest of foods*; with singing lips my mouth will praise you (Psalm 63:4–5, italics mine).

The Bible is filled with pictures of fullness. Jesus' promise is consistent with the biblical ideal of being satisfied in our relationship with God.

Jesus promised us we would not just get morsels of God if we hunger for Him. He said we would push away from the table stuffed with His righteousness! The Bible reminds us that the nature of the kingdom of heaven is really not about physical food but feasting on the righteousness of God (Romans 14:17). And, through our relationship with Christ, that righteousness secured for us through His death, burial, and resurrection will be abundantly more than we need to be made right with Holy God. We are filled and free to pursue the life He has for us until He returns. When Jesus revealed the truth that He was the One His followers were longing for and that He would fulfill their deepest desires, He wasn't just speaking to those actually standing in His physical presence; He was making a promise for all that would follow them and that would stand for all eternity.

The Illness

Have you ever eaten something just because it looked appealing? You weren't even really very hungry but you walk into the house and the smell of freshly baked oatmeal cookies meets you head on. Ten minutes later you've downed five cookies and a jumbo glass of milk. You do the math in your head and soon realize it would take you three hours on the treadmill to offset what you just slammed down in a few minutes. Regret, remorse, and "what was I thinking?" fill your sugar-buzzed brain.

Hunger and thirst are messages our organs send to our brain signaling the need for replenishment. Unfortunately, most of us at one time or another have either ignored or overridden these signals, sometimes intentionally, sometimes not. When we distort these God-given needs and satisfy them with things that are not healthy, we can harm ourselves. This is the case when we overindulge *and* under consume. Obesity, anorexia, and bulimia are all prevalent illnesses in today's culture that stem from improperly satisfying our natural, God-given hunger and thirst for food and water.

Spiritually, we do the same sort of thing. For those of us who are Christians, I believe spiritual malnutrition is evidence that we have not spent sufficient time with Jesus. Those who have not trusted Christ will never find real satisfaction until they trust Him. They will seek to fill their emptiness with things that do not satisfy until they trust Christ as their Lord and Savior. Spiritual hunger can only be satisfied through a relationship with Christ.

People attempt to fill their spiritual hunger with activity, adventure, success, wealth, happiness, food, entertainment, and a variety of other things, but none of them wholly and completely satisfy.

God embedded within the software of all creation a 24-hour rest period.

Only the Bread of life (John 6:35) and Living Water (John 4:13–14) will put an end to spiritual hunger pangs.

Spiritual illness results when we seek to solve our spiritual hunger with *un*spiritual things. Religious activity, believe it or not, may be a symptom of spiritual illness. I have little doubt you can think of someone (or several people) who are at church every time the church doors are open. While outwardly such involvement seems admirable, there must certainly be needs going unmet at home and in integral relationships. There are simply not enough hours in the day or week to tend to all of life's responsibilities *and* be at church for every available activity. Something eventually suffers.

Religion is the outward actions of your inward relationship with God. Sick religion is caring more about your outward appearance as a religious person than about your personal relationship with God. Jesus warned against such activity (Matthew 6:1–8), and we are to avoid such behavior in our journey toward spiritual wellness.

See if you recognize some of the following physical symptoms as they relate to spiritual health:

Shortness of breath—this indicates you are able to spend only a minute or two in prayer at a time; wandering thoughts and a short-lived attention span are key characteristics.

Spiritual obesity—this symptom occurs when you spend too much time in religious activity at the church so that you have no time to minister to those Jesus has called you to serve. Other symptoms include knowing more names of church friends than those without Christ or spending more time at potluck dinners at church than at neighborhood block parties to meet your neighbors.

High blood pressure—this is a result of trying to maintain a schedule so full of activities that you simply can't find the time to seek out quiet places to build your relationship with God.

Clogged arteries—these occur when you have eaten from the plate of entertainment and drunk from the cup of pleasure to the point that your spiritual veins are virtually impassable. When *you* can't receive and enjoy the life-giving presence of the Holy Spirit, you can't pass it on to others.

High cholesterol—if you eat more fatty spiritual food, spoon-fed to you by others, than you work off through exercising your heart and mind to study God's Word on your own, your blood tests will reflect dangerous levels.

All of us are deficient in one or more of these areas at different stages of our life. Maybe a houseful of toddlers makes it just about impossible to spend more than fleeting moments in prayer. Maybe you've spent so many nights entertaining clients that you've forgotten the joy of a night home with your kids. Or, maybe the Tuesday morning women's Bible study teacher is so good you've signed up for her Thursday night class and weekend retreat despite your husband's discouragement. The important thing is to evaluate where you stand in these areas from time to time. Take stock of where and how you spend your time in relation to God, family, friends, and what you consider to be your area of personal ministry. Just as addressing physical ills early on is beneficial, so also is it of tremendous benefit to treat a spiritual ailment early.

The Exercise

I've got a radical challenge for you. If you're truly intent on experiencing authentic hunger and thirst for God's consuming presence in your life, consider this: *Sabbath rest*. The only way we can satisfy our spiritual hunger and thirst is by making time for our relationship with God and making it a priority. We can't begin to experience Jesus' promise until we learn to exercise letting Him become our source of spiritual nourishment.

Since the very first days of creation, God ordained a day of rest. Think about that. God created the entire universe and all that is within it in six days and on the seventh, He rested. Don't you think He could have used that extra day to maybe polish up a few rough edges? Maybe if He had clocked in on that extra day, He could have addressed Eve's questionable integrity. Maybe He could have shored up Adam's resolve to "just say no!" Or, maybe Adam and Eve could have busied themselves like the rest of us—at the mall, rearranging the den, or cleaning out the garage instead of sneaking in that deadly snack.

But God *didn't* work on the seventh day. It wasn't some oversight. He didn't oversleep. He didn't consider going into the office for "just a few hours." It was deliberate and intentional and meant to be the example for all of us to follow. Sabbath rest is literally God-ordained. God embedded within the software of all creation a 24-hour rest period after every six consecutive days. God believed Sabbath rest to be significant enough to make it one of the ten indisputable guidelines for living and tells us so:

> *Remember the Sabbath day by keeping it holy.*
>
> —EXODUS 20:8

He did this because the Sabbath was designed to be *the* day when all could rest from work and worship the Source of life.

Jesus also affirmed the principle of the Sabbath when the religious leaders challenged Him as to its nature and purpose (Matthew 12:1–14).

The Sabbath is also a metaphor for of our salvation. The opening verses of Hebrews 4 draw the parallels completely, but it can be summed up in these few verses:

> *There remains, then, a Sabbath-rest for the people of God; for anyone who enters God's rest also rests from his own work, just as God did from his. Let us, therefore, make every effort to enter that rest, so that no one will fall by following their example of disobedience.*
>
> —HEBREWS 4:9–11

Sabbath rest is undeniably part of God's plan for all He created. To disregard it or to deny it is to refuse to trust how God created all things.

Why Sabbath rest?

Sabbath rest is ultimately an act of trust in God. When we refuse to work for 24 hours, we dethrone the god of self-effort and we trust that God will provide without our hard work. Sabbath rest allows our body, soul, and mind to rest from the daily pull of life. Client demands are set aside for the day. Social obligations can be met another time. And maintaining the race from soccer practice to math tutoring to dinner from the drive-through will all resume soon enough. Sabbath rest is a means of hitting the pause button on our surplus of responsibilities, our obligations outside the needs of our immediate family, and endless opportunities for distraction. Twenty-four hours of broken routine allows God to be our source of strength and nourishment. These every-seventh-day breaks protect us from filling our spiritual hunger and thirst with things other than our relationship with God. The Sabbath principle is God's gracious offering to us to keep us vitally engaged with Him. *Sabbath rest is an aid station on our journey to spiritual wellness.* If we fail to stop and receive the aid Christ offers, we will perish spiritually.

When I run an ultramarathon, any distance over the marathon length of 26.2 miles, aid stations are an essential part of a strategy to finish. Fuel and hydration are key factors in running on trails between six and eight hours or longer. If the race director has placed the stations effectively, runners can plan to refuel and replenish their water supply between stretches of terrain carrying only what they can use efficiently. Bananas, cookies, corn chips, oranges, peanut butter sandwiches, and

assorted trail mixes and candies are a runner's oasis when his or her body has used up all its reserves. Leaving with handfuls or pockets full of food and bottles or backpacks full of water allows the runner to survive the next leg of the run. Some aid stations on longer runs provide chairs and places to lay down to rest in order to keep the runner going. Sabbath rest is to our physical and spiritual ultramarathon of life what an aid station is to an ultramarathoner.

As is always the case in something He ordained, God took care of all the provisions regarding the Sabbath. He even scheduled it in for us on creation's calendar. And, just for the record, He *inked* it in! For Christian's, Sunday is our day of worship and rest. However, as our everyday existence has become increasingly more global in nature and as many of us assume a nontraditional Monday through Friday school and workweek, it has become *even more* crucial to designate a specific day *in advance* each week that you proclaim as your *personal day of rest*. Whatever day you choose in a seven-day cycle, it needs to be clear of clutter, removed from the daily tasks that normally consume you, and enjoyed as a time of revitalizing physically, emotionally, and spiritually.

If the thought of going cold turkey in your all-out pursuit of a restful Sabbath leaves you completely freaked out, you're like most on-the-go, gotta-get-it-done Americans.

"What about the weekly stock-up trip to Target?"

"What if I don't get those expense reports totaled by Monday morning?"

"But it's a *tournament*—not just a regular soccer game!"

Hey, I hear you. I've spent Sunday afternoons at Walmart getting science fair supplies just like you and Sunday evenings stewing over my next week's calendar wondering how I would fit it all in. Carving a genuine Sabbath out of an already packed schedule is difficult. Mark Buchanan reflects on why Sabbath rest is so important:

> Indeed, this is the essence of a Sabbath rest: paying attention. It is being fully present, wholly awake, in each moment. It is the trained ability to inhabit our own existence without reminder, so that even the simplest things . . . gain the force of discovery and revelation. True attention burns away the layers of indifference and ennui and distraction.[4]

Without margin to pay attention to ourselves or to God, we will be left to our own devices to handle what life hands us. We must practice Sabbath rest to have the time to pay attention.

Consider the following plan I alluded to earlier to schedule the Sabbath principle into your lifestyle:

Divert daily—Find 20 minutes every day to feast on the Bread of life through Bible study or drink from the Living Water through prayer.

Withdraw weekly—Take one day away from work to experience a Sabbath rest of trust in God. Include worship and fellowship with others who, like you, are on a spiritual journey with Jesus.

Quit quarterly—Every three months take a two-day retreat from your routine to evaluate where you have been and where you are going. Allow God to steer you to and keep you on the mission He has called you to accomplish.

Abandon annually—If possible, take an extended vacation from work and the pressures of your lifestyle, a time in which you idle your mind, rest your body, and refresh your soul through recreation, study, and rest.

Sabbath rest is a spiritual discipline that will allow God to satisfy your hunger and thirst for Him in ways that will rejuvenate you mentally, physically, emotionally, and especially spiritually.

Takeaway

This fourth beatitude is pivotal because, up till now, the previous verses were more descriptions of emptiness and usually not tops on our lists of preferred feelings. They serve their purpose, though, as necessary precursors to this fourth, exceedingly more hopeful verse which promises fullness—the fullness we all long for in our souls. What's more, this fullness is twofold: initially and continually. When we accept Christ and when we continue to seek Him, we are filled to overflowing with His glory. When we take time for a Sabbath rest, feast on God's presence, and drink of His Spirit, Jesus promises we will be satisfied and changed. For the better. Forever.

We've reached the summit on our journey to spiritual wellness. Naturally, most of us would like to pitch a tent, build a fire, and set up camp. And you can . . . for a while. But because so much of life happens in the valley of our days, it's our responsibility as those who have reached the summit to retreat and equip others for the journey upward. Assuming at this point that you have been filled with the things of God, it is now time for Him to accompany you into the valley of relationships to bring peace to others. When God fills you with His righteousness, this becomes a privilege and an opportunity, not an obligation. Because of the transformation you've allowed God to take place within you, your behavior will lead you to act rightly; you'll respond with merciful actions, pure motives, and efforts to bring peace to all your relationships. These are exciting and challenging stops on this journey to spiritual wellness, but well worth the adventure.

Questions for Reflection

1. With what do you fill your natural hunger and thirst? Would you label your choices healthy?

2. What about your emotional and spiritual hungers? How do you fill them?

3. Which description of righteousness struck you as what you needed to know now? Have you accepted the righteousness God offers you in Christ Jesus through trusting in Him?

4. Do you practice a Sabbath rest? If so, describe some of your practices here. If not, what are some things you can do to make margin for this spiritual practice? What suggestions in this chapter could you use to make your Sabbath rest more effective?

CHAPTER 7

The Merciful

Blessed are the merciful, for they will be shown mercy.

—Matthew 5:7

I love the Old Testament story of Joseph. An arrogant teenager with good looks and visions of grandeur, Joseph drove his jealous brothers crazy with his overflowing self-confidence (Genesis 37:3–9). Can't you just see a smart-aleck kid tagging after his older brothers wherever they went? Not only did he follow his brothers *everywhere* they went, but he constantly trash-talked them, going on and on about how someday . . . *someday they* would be tailing him and wanting *his* approval rather than how it was at the moment. In one especially emboldened moment, Joseph went so far as to describe his dreams to them, complete with endearing details that involved *their* grain sheaves bowing down to *his harvest*. And, as if adding insult to injury, he also mentioned the sun, the stars, and the moon would be in on the bowing action too.

And then, as only big brothers can do, one of them probably grabbed him and put him in a half nelson neck-hold while the others gave him a now-you'll-be-singing-soprano wedgie. Then, I figure they dropped him to the ground, kicked some dirt his way, and told him to keep his stupid dreams to himself if he knew what was good for him. They finally had enough and after intervention by Reuben, the oldest, they sold him to a caravan headed for Egypt to get him out of their hair.

OK, so I added a bit of color commentary, but that *is* the gist of the story. Joseph did have the two dreams, and his brothers did tell him to 'knock it off' in so many Hebrew words. Then, through circumstances beyond Joseph's control, God tamed his inflated self-image, knocked him down a few dozen notches, and made him a living, breathing, class A example of what it means to be meek. Once Joseph embraced his newfound alter ego, the Lord once again intervened in Joseph's life and cast him in a series of positions that ultimately led to him becoming the second most powerful man in the world.

The climax of the story came as Joseph's brothers came

looking for food. They stumbled into Egypt from Canaan and by the time they arrived, Joseph was Pharaoh's right-hand man, having helped Egypt not just to survive but actually flourish during the time of worldwide famine. When the desperate band of brothers came before him, Joseph recognized the men as his brothers who had hated him so much they had years before conspired to kill him. He then had a choice to make: he could use his power and position to repay their unkindness to them, or he could use his advantage to preserve his family.

Joseph chose mercy over revenge and his family was blessed because of it. Had he chosen revenge over mercy, it would have destroyed all that God had orchestrated as His plan for His people. Fortunately for the sake of his family lineage and for the purposes of God, Joseph

> The word mercy is often equated with weakness.

was able to see the work of God above the hurtful schemes of others. He confessed, "But God sent me ahead of you to preserve for you a remnant on earth and to save your lives by a great deliverance" (Genesis 45:7).

Mercy in Your Life

We can show mercy toward others like Joseph when we have personally encountered a hunger-and-thirst-after-righteousness experience with God. It doesn't necessarily have to be a dramatic emotional experience, but rather an honest, heart-rending encounter with God that changes our lives—*forever*. And just as we grow in our relationship with God through progressive experiences with Him, we also stand to grow similarly as we regularly and repeatedly focus on living out the beatitudes in our daily lives. It's not a one-time read-through where you familiarize yourself with the general principles of Christ's sermon and move on from there. In fact, it is nothing of the sort.

All is fine and good most of the time, you say, but Thanksgiving with the in-laws . . . that's another story! And don't even ask me about the office know-it-all who crosses all sorts of politically incorrect boundaries! Or my obnoxious neighbor who's the self-appointed enforcer when it comes to HOA code violations! Or the . . .

Hold up, my friend, and read on to discover how Christ empowers all of us in the most trying of times to show mercy to others. This herculean, yeah-but-you-don't-know-*my*-family task begins with making serious inroads into becoming merciful . . . even with your brother-in-law . . . and beyond that bothersome lady in the cubicle next to yours . . . and the neighbor who doesn't shovel his dog's "business" when he stops in your yard.

The People

Jesus said, "Blessed are the merciful, for they will be shown mercy" (Matthew 5:7). Like *meekness*, the word *mercy* is often equated with weakness. Persons who show mercy, forgiveness, and love toward those who have offended them sometimes look weak. The world's wisdom would say *if someone offends you, you deserve to get revenge any way you can!* Never before has the "eye for an eye" mentality been as prevalent in culture as it is today. Many blame the distressing economic times, bitterly divided political climate, and the entitlement mentality as the primary factors that have all contributed to this self-centered, self-focused mind-set so many maintain in their personal and professional relationships. But, do you want to know the irony of this thinking? These same issues were present when Jesus gave this message. There were clashing economic classes. Rival rulers spent their days plotting the demise of those they considered enemies, and many were convinced their existence was, quite literally, the very center of the universe. What Jesus said to His followers resonates just as clearly today, "Blessed are the merciful."

Jesus blessed those who forgave. He knew those who were merciful have tender hearts that then translates into the ability to gently lead others to God's merciful heart. Jesus taught that a forgiven heart would be a forgiving heart; those who knew God's mercy would show that same mercy to others.

WHEN GIVEN MERCY, SHARE MERCY

In Matthew 18:23–35 Jesus told a story of a king who decided to settle his accounts with his servants. When he realized one of them could not pay the huge amount owed, he ordered the

> Jesus' death, burial, and resurrection are mercy incarnate.

man and his family thrown into jail. However, when the servant begged the king for patience until he paid his debt, the king had compassion on his servant, canceled his debt, and let him go. On the way home the forgiven servant ran into a fellow servant who owed him little more than pocket change compared to the debt he was just forgiven. In what could only be described as short-term memory failure, the forgiven man grabbed the one who owed him and began to choke him, demanding payment immediately. When the indebted servant begged for patience, the forgiven servant callously refused and had the man thrown in jail.

When the other servants heard about this incident, they told the king. He called the forgiven servant into his chambers and asked him, "Shouldn't you have had mercy on your fellow servant just as I had on you?" (v. 33). Mercy in this verse means just what it meant in the Beatitudes—*forgiveness.*

Obviously the responsibility to pass on the mercy shown to the forgiven servant was lost on him. It's a safe bet he had plenty of time to ponder this responsibility to reciprocate when the king had him thrown into prison until all his debts were satisfied in full. Jesus took this teachable moment to make a significant point with His disciples when He explained, "This is how my heavenly Father will treat each of you unless you forgive your brother from your heart" (18:35).

At the heart of Jesus' lesson is how His followers are to give and receive mercy. Jesus showed how those who have received mercy should show others the same forgiveness. God's forgiveness of our sins is the standard by which we forgive others (Colossians 3:13). Jesus blesses those who show mercy because, in doing so, they reveal the heart of God. He knows our ability to forgive is directly related to our sense of being forgiven. It's kind of like Jesus saying, "Congratulations for showing my mercy to others; I've got plenty more where that came from and I'll share it with *you*."

The Characteristic

Mercy describes the heart of God. Mercy is at the center of the good news. Mercy satisfies a debt we cannot pay that is forgiven by the One we owe. We are in spiritual debt to God because of our sin. We have no way to repay what we owe (Romans 3:23) and we deserve death (Romans 6:23) for it. But because God loves us so much, He allowed His Son to die in our place to pay our debt (Romans 5:8). As holy and righteous God, He can separate us eternally from Himself, but His mercy drives Him to forgive us if we will receive His payment for our debt. We are not and cannot be saved by anything we do, but rather by the mercy of God (Titus 3:5). Jesus blessed those who showed mercy because they demonstrated the love of God.

Nowhere are we more like God than when we show mercy to others. By extending mercy, we are offering forgiveness to the guilty as well as compassion for the suffering.

THOSE FORGIVEN MUCH LOVE MORE

The story in Luke 7:36–50 tells of the woman who bathed Jesus' feet with her tears and expensive perfume as He sat in the home of a notable Pharisee. When the presumably elite of the group questioned the worthiness and significance of the woman's actions, Jesus quickly came to her defense. He saw in her actions a heart that was changed because she had been forgiven. The Pharisee, however, saw only a woman "who had lived a sinful life" (7:37). The religious leader couldn't see beyond her social status and, sadly, refused to grant her mercy. Then Jesus went about explaining that those who realize how much they have been forgiven are able to love much, but those who have only been forgiven little, love little. The same concept is true for mercy: mercy *received* breeds mercy *given.*

Mercy should also be the motivation for our actions toward those who are hungry, in prison, or without clothes (Matthew 25:31–46). Jesus scolded the religious leaders who kept the rules about tithing but forgot the bigger issues of judgment, *mercy,* and faith (Matthew 23:23)—a classic case of not being able to see the forest of mercy for the trees of religion.

In the battle of big picture things versus daily details, mercy is not just *a* big picture item for Christ followers; it is *the* big picture when it comes to honoring Christ. God's ultimate demonstration of mercy to us cost Him His son. Jesus' death, burial, and resurrection are *mercy incarnate.* At the very least, as disciples of Jesus, extending mercy to others should be a consistent goal in our lives.

A GIFT OF THE SPIRIT

Mercy is also a gift of the Holy Spirit (Romans 12:8). If mercy is the heart of God and spiritual gifts are manifestations of the Spirit of God in a disciple's life, then mercy would be chief among those gifts. In practical terms, I describe the gift this way: "Cheerful acts of compassion characterize those with the gift of mercy. Persons with this gift aid the body by empathizing with hurting members. They keep the body healthy and unified by keeping others aware of the needs within the church."[1]

God gifts members of the church with the spiritual ability to empathize with those who need forgiveness and who are hurting. These are the people who are always drawn to providing relief, comfort, and resources to those in times of sorrow, loss, and despair. Sometimes this manifests itself as a hearty homemade meal for those grieving the loss of a loved one. Other times it means shepherding a fellow sinner through a valley of addiction, relationship discord, or childhood rebellion because you've traveled a similar path in your past. And still other times it can mean giving an able-bodied person a chance at a job and the dignity that comes from working. It can play out in a million different ways when those filled with the spiritual gift of mercy are prompted to serve. These members are like the heart of a person that moves him or her to help someone in need. They become advocates for the weak and are ready to forgive quickly those who offend them.

The Promise

Mercy comes with a promise. Jesus said, "Blessed are the merciful, *for they will be shown mercy*" (Matthew 5:7, italics mine). This is the only verse in this passage where Christ's promise is the same as the condition He congratulates. To show mercy is to receive mercy. As we grow in our understanding of mercy, the more inclined we are to show it to others, and the more we show mercy, the more mercy is heaped upon us. It's a concept that goes against our natural way of thinking because it is counterintuitive to the way much of the world operates in business, relationships, and even in some church-related efforts.

When we demonstrate mercy to others, we are right in the middle of where God wants us to be. We're like a living, breathing conduit of mercy. Mercy goes out to those in my life; mercy comes in from Christ. It's a terrific word picture that illustrates the cyclical nature of the Beatitudes. For us to ensure mercy is continually flowing in and through us, we have to perpetually return to the summit of our relationship with God and feast at His table of righteousness.

It is important to understand that Jesus' promise does *not* guarantee you will receive mercy every time you offer mercy to others—at least not in terms of what we consider acceptable. *Your motivation for being merciful cannot be rooted in expectations of reciprocal feelings.* It must be grounded in obedience to the challenge of Christ, to do as He commands and not to receive something in return from others. Be warned; sometimes we show mercy only to be greeted by further offenses or total ingratitude. If that happens to you, you're in good company. Jesus also lived among the ungrateful.

Luke 17:11–18 tells how Jesus healed ten men suffering from the horrors of leprosy and told them to go and show themselves healed to their priests. Of the ten, only one returned to give thanks to Jesus. He asked that man, "Were not all ten cleansed? Where are the other nine? Was no one found to return and give praise to God except this foreigner?" (vv. 17–18). Hard to imagine, isn't it? You're dying a slow, painful death; you're ostracized by society and forced to live among the graves of the already dead, and yet by the kindness of a stranger you're miraculously and completely

Joy flows from mercy.

healed, and yet you can't manage a return trip to say thanks? Unbelievable, but all too often true.

Take comfort in knowing that you can count on receiving mercy from God when you demonstrate His heart to others; just don't hold your breath when it comes to receiving praise from others. Give mercy without expectations. You may be met with appreciation, reconciliation, and gratitude. Or you may not. However, one thing is for sure: you *will* bring honor to the One who first showed *you* mercy. And that's not just a promise; that's a *forever* promise.

The Illness

If mercy gets out of balance, it can cause us to carry the burdens of others—many others—as our own. And while that may seem admirably helpful, if not sacrificial at first glance, it can have disastrous results. Because mercy allows us to empathize with others in their pain and/or sin, it often motivates us to act on behalf of that person, and that is not a healthy condition for either party. This is why, I believe, Paul exhorted those with the spiritual gift of mercy to exercise it "cheerfully" (Romans 12:8). Too much involvement in a person's need can lead to negative attitudes toward them and others.

It's not surprising that, as a pastor, I've seen this occur all too frequently in a congregation full of mercy-filled, well-meaning people who are intent on becoming the hands and feet of Jesus so much as they are able. The problem arises when the outreach becomes overwhelming, all-consuming, and results in neglect to other, equally viable, priorities.

Such a scenario happened between two families, both with ten-year-old little girls. When the Marcuses' daughter, Olivia, was diagnosed with childhood leukemia, her best friend's family, the Jacksons, were the first to respond to all sorts of needs. Delivering meals, running errands, and tending to household and yard-related maintenance issues became second nature for the Jacksons as they watched their dear friends endure the challenges of a seriously ill child.

These acts of service went on for a couple of months before things reached a tipping point at the Jackson home. Whereas once their children were the priority of the evening, tending to the details of Marcuses' house had become more important to Tom and Sandy Jackson. Keeping *their* pantry stocked, *their* lawn mowed, and *their* car repaired soon took precedence over the responsibilities at the Jackson home. The frustrations felt among the Jackson family members (both between each other and toward the Marcuses) went unspoken and unaddressed.

When the doctor ordered six more months of extensive treatment, despair set in at the Jackson house—first, for what this meant for Olivia and secondly, for the extended upheaval that was sure to follow at their own house. That is, until husband, father, and spiritual leader of the Jackson family, Tom, made a preemptive decision. He reestablished his family as *the* priority for him and his wife and, in doing so, was able to restore normalcy, regularity, and value to *their* family.

Yes, it was heartbreaking what the Marcuses were going through. Yes, it was Tom Jackson's and his family's privilege and responsibility to minister to them in their time of need. And yes, sacrificing for and enduring a little discomfort for others was a valuable lesson for his kids, but . . . the line had long since been crossed that separated Christian service, brotherly love, and empathetic outreach from what his family had provided. So much so, that he couldn't remember the last time his family—just his family—had *all* been together at one time. The Jacksons are a classic example of what can happen when we take carrying other's burdens to an extreme.

JOY IS THE BY-PRODUCT OF MERCY

One of the natural by-products of this amazing gift of mercy is joy. Once we move past the mourning of our condition, joy is the next inevitable emotion. Hear the words of the psalmist as he recounts the complete 180 turn his life took upon accepting Christ's indescribable gift:

> *Hear, O Lord, and be merciful to me. . . . You turned my wailing into dancing; you removed my sackcloth and clothed me with joy*
>
> —Psalm 30:10–11

This guy experienced an amazing transformation. He went from weeping to dancing and from ashes and sackcloth to garments of joy! That's not just a made-the-red-light, got-a-great-review, hallelujah-it's-chicken-fried-steak-night praise; that's a seismic shift in perspective from some seriously deep depression to shout-it-from-the-mountaintop elation. And it all stemmed from God's gift of mercy.

Remember this next time you're tempted to rush full speed ahead into solving and resolving other people's problems. *Joy flows from mercy*. It is not killed because of it. Few things kill joy quicker, faster, and more decisively than trying to carry a burden someone else should be carrying. It is important for each of us always to be mindful that our help should never interfere with allowing others the opportunity to retain their own individual responsibilities.

Working as a community provides the safeguard to overload that exercising mercy may bring to a person's life. By living together as a family of God, those who are able carry those who are in need of Jesus' mercy. And, just as major life events occur for each of us, this responsibility to carry others also continually shifts, allowing for restoration when needed and opportunity for service when renewed. The ultimate remedy, however, for the weary warriors of mercy is found in Jesus' promise: those who show mercy will be shown mercy by God and those in service with them.

The Exercise

The ability to show mercy is a by-product of God's transforming presence in your life. You can't manufacture it on your own, it is evidence of the Holy Spirit's reign in your heart, but you can nurture this characteristic so you can show mercy to the persons God places in your life.

One reason you may not eagerly show mercy to others is that you feel you don't have the time it takes to demonstrate it fully to them. You know that showing mercy involves more than simply saying, "You are forgiven. Go, now, and get over your sin!" Or, as the techno-generation calls it, "slacktivism," which means to click a "like" button on Facebook or to retweet a message or link in order to engage "socially in activism that requires little or no effort as part of a lifestyle or self-identity."[2] Mercy takes more time and energy than forwarding an email to your friends.

What I've discovered throughout my ministry is that *simplicity is the spiritual exercise that can best assist us in making room in order to experience mercy and to show it to others.* By simplifying our lifestyles, we're more flexible and thus, we can be more accommodating with our time and services. Simplicity of lifestyle affords us more time free of obligations and less time required to manage the stuff in our lives.

Besides diminishing (or totally eliminating!) our inclination and opportunity for honoring Christ's call to be merciful, our overcommitted, double-booked, caffeine-fueled sprint through the days, weeks, and years of our lives prohibit us from finding time to experience God's mercy in our own lives. How sad that oftentimes the very people whom Christ has selected to receive and give His mercy are the ones so consumed with their own stuff that they have no time for others.

CHECK YOUR CALENDAR AND CHECKBOOK FOR CLUES

I have found one way to gain a better perspective of where the hours and minutes of my day escape is to look back at my calendar for the week. In doing so, I have to keep in mind that even the slightest commitments almost always take longer than I initially expect.

Consider this example: Let's say soccer practice is Tuesdays 5:00–6:00. No big deal; it's only an hour. Ah, but wait. It's your day to drive to practice and in order to get everyone there by 5:00, you've got to leave at 4:15 to pick up Jake, Luke, and Steven. You pull into the soccer complex at 4:55, unload the kids, and the coach flags you down—just to give you a friendly reminder that it's your day to bring snacks for the whole group. Next stop, the grocery store. Precut fruit, juice boxes, one overpriced, out-of-season cooler, and two bags of ice. Check, check, check, and check. But wait—shouldn't you pick up something for dinner while you're here? Definitely . . . except that it's 5:50 and you've got to head back to the soccer fields. By the time you unload and distribute the snacks and reload and distribute the carpool kids, it's coming up on 6:45. You're still in your work clothes, have no plans or provisions for dinner, and you've got to help your fourth grader build a replica of the Coliseum. You push #6 on speed dial and order "the usual" from Domino's. Mercy? "*Mercy me!*" is all you can mumble as you nod off before the local news.

If you're really serious about ending a cycle such as this, take the time to *review your last month's calendar*. Count the number of discretionary activities you and your family participated in and all the ancillary responsibilities that accompanied them (parent meetings, fund-raisers, special projects). Now count the number of activities that help to bring you and your family closer to God. There it is—conviction courtesy of *your* own calendar.

Can you handle one more hit-you-where-you-live personal accountability indicator? *Scroll through your checkbook register or online debit statement*. Mark the expenditures that were an investment in people and projects that will yield eternal value. Dry cleaners? Not so much. Haircut? No, again. New pair of running shoes? Doubtful. Once again, conviction—this time courtesy of your dollars and cents.

Where you consistently spend your time and resources is a direct reflection of where you place your priorities. To be sure, there are some commitments and expenses that are just part of everyday life; and there are some involvements and some purchases that are just outright enjoyable and you shouldn't necessarily berate yourself for those either. However, if over the course of a month you see few, if any, time commitments or financial resources invested in things eternal in nature, it may be time to reevaluate what you consider to be your priorities. If you say something is important and yet your actions don't back it up, either your priorities are out of line or they're really not priorities. Please understand that I'm not trying to send you packing on an all-expenses-paid guilt trip. I just want you to be able to see things as they *really are*, not how you *say* you would like them to be.

Taking this gut-check inventory is not the brainchild of some hard-core theologians intended to coerce believers into abandoning all forms of enjoyment in lieu of joyless service to others. The challenge to honestly evaluate how we spend our time and money comes directly from Christ Himself:

> *But seek first his kingdom and his righteousness, and all these things* [food, clothing, and shelter] *will be given to you as well.*
>
> —MATTHEW 6:33 (BRACKETED WORDS MINE)

The people who follow Jesus' teaching "easily put all demands that come to them in 'their place' and deal harmoniously, peacefully, and confidently with complexities of life that seem incomprehensible to others, for they know what they are doing . . . simplicity makes great complexity bearable."[3] You must seek kingdom things before you pursue earthly stuff in order to allow the priority of showing mercy to make its way into your lifestyle. To put the kingdom of God first takes your focus from keeping up with the Joneses to living out the characteristics of God.

A WORKOUT PLAN FOR SIMPLICITY

I have put together a few simple exercises to help you practice this concept of simplicity in your daily life.

1. Place all of your legally binding papers (contracts, wills, powers of attorney) that assign ownership to you on a table and pray over them. A possible prayer might sound like, "God, You own these. I simply manage them for You. Please give me the wisdom to use them to build Your kingdom."
2. Ask God to reveal any addictions you have—things such as watching too much television, surfing the Internet, or consuming caffeine or sugar. Address these addictions one at a time by fasting from them for a season. Use your newfound time to serve others. Allow the removal of the behavior to make you more sensitive to the feelings of others.
3. Refuse to buy any new clothes for a month. Instead, clean out your closets and give away those items you have not worn in the last year.
4. This week schedule ten minutes a day as an appointment with God. Extend that time if God leads you to do so.
5. Seek out one person who needs to be shown the mercy of God. Allow God to help you demonstrate His mercy in that individual's life. Commit to doing that action for a given period of time.

As you draw closer to God, you will find other ways to exercise the discipline of simplicity. Remember that you do this to make more room in your lifestyle for those who need to know the mercy God has shown you. You do not simplify your life to meet some legalistic assignment. The joy God brings to your life will provide motivation for your actions.

Takeaway

Jesus blesses you when you show others mercy. When you show others Christlike mercy you demonstrate that His Spirit is transforming you into a kingdom person. Jesus' promise to you is that when you show mercy you will be shown mercy. God's mercy never fails.

We are on our descent into the valley of relationships. We have climbed the slopes of spiritual poverty, repentance, and meekness, and we have been on the summit and experienced the righteousness of God. That fulfillment has begun to show itself in our changed hearts and in our actions toward others. Our next stop on our journey to wellness is becoming "pure in heart"—a tremendously important trait that will affect our relationship with God and with others.

Questions for Reflection

1. Have you experienced the forgiving mercy of God? If so, describe that experience or series of events to a friend or record them in a journal. If not, reread the section, "The Characteristic," and consider what God offers you through His mercy demonstrated in His Son Jesus' love.

2. Have you experienced mercy shown to you by others? Describe that experience and how it made you feel.

3. List some reasons why it is difficult for you to demonstrate godlike mercy to others? Be honest.

4. What are some of your first responses to the suggestions related to the spiritual exercise of simplicity? Do your calendar and checkbook tell the story of someone who gladly shows mercy and serves others?

CHAPTER 8

The Pure in Heart

Blessed are the pure in heart, for they will see God.

—Matthew 5:8

A young wife and mother visited our church one Sunday when I preached on the importance of Christ followers maintaining a single-minded devotion to God. Despite a constant soundtrack of conflict, calamity, and worry in her life, the words stuck and proved to be an-impossible-to-dismiss echo in her heart. She stopped by my office later in the week to tell me about the impact the message from God's Word had upon her disjointed and disheveled life. "Your sermon really spoke to me," she began. "I have a lot of trouble making room for God in my life. My family is always in a crisis—just this week my younger sister told us she is pregnant with her second child and that she's not sure who the father is. Her first child has a different bio-dad and is only four months old. My husband works extremely long hours and wasn't able to come with me on Sunday because he was called in."

She paused for a moment as if to decide whether to finish telling me of other trials in her life that were simultaneously reaching critical mass, but she continued, "I'm an apartment manager, and because of a nearby plant layoff, we've got lots of vacancies now. The complex was even up for sale, but now the buyers have backed off. Every day I get more and more pressure to get the units filled. I plan to keep coming to church no matter what though. I know I need God in my life, but sometimes He just seems to get lost in the shuffle."

Her words were both compelling and convicting to me. Sure, I had plenty of demands on my time, more bills than I would have preferred, and a honey-do list that I never quite seemed to get to the bottom of but, by and large, my daily challenges weren't anywhere near the stress level of hers. And yet I too have allowed God "*to get lost in the shuffle.*" Here I was, a so-called professional when it came to speaking about God, having only a spattering of the same issues as this overworked, overloaded, and overstressed young wife and mother juggling family issues, job hardships, and financial difficulties. If I, with my mostly mundane, run-of-the-mill, standard life issues, wrestled with all-in devotion to God, was there any hope for this young woman to find the time to contemplate reaching a place of single-minded devotion to God?

Mercifully for both of us, the answer was a resounding "Yes!" Though it is all too easy to become consumed with the messes and mistakes of our lives and be tempted to throw in the towel regarding our questionable worth, God looks past the poor choices, disastrous results, and desperate measures we all take on at some point in our lives. Mercifully, He looks straight into our hearts to understand our true motives. From God's perspective, *pure motives trump miscalculated and messed up outcomes every time.*

Can you identify with my occasional weak-willed devotion to God? Do you see bits of yourself in situations similar to the young mom? Do you find it nearly impossible to complete a simple prayer without some outside concern interrupting your time with God? Have you ever experienced a prayer like this?

> Dear Lord,
>
> *Thank You for this glorious day and the wonderful rain You've brought our way* (gotta remember to turn off the sprinkler system!). *We praise You for our family, friends* (remember the Millers' barbecue at 5:00 today; don't forget the potato salad), *and church* (budget meeting, 4:00 this afternoon). *We lift up the prayer requests of those shared today* (Is Mrs. Johnson *ever* going to quit sharing all her ailments?) *and those unspoken requests. We trust You to take care of our needs and know that all good things come from Your generous provision in our lives.* (Is that dentist appointment tomorrow at 11:00 or next Monday at 11:00? Where did I put that reminder card?) *We ask all this in Your most holy name.*
>
> Amen.

If your life is anything like mine, you can easily identify with this age-old struggle to maintain focus on just one thing. The sad and pathetic irony of our struggle is what should be the easiest thing on earth to dwell upon is oftentimes the hardest and easiest to neglect. Demanding preschoolers, get-it-done-or-else bosses, and sometimes insensitive spouses all have a way of getting our attention more often and more readily than the One who gave us life. Talk about misplaced priorities! And yet, this oneness of focus, this complete devotion, and this single-mindedness of soul is what Christ desires in exchange for His blessing. It is precisely what He meant when He said, "Blessed are the pure in heart, for they will see God" (Matthew 5:8). Jesus blessed those who knew the one thing they were created for and were doing it in relationship with Him.

What Does *Pure in Heart* Mean, Anyway?

Who are the "pure in heart"? One translation notes that the word *single* (KJV) or *good* (NIV) means "simple, single, clear, healthy or sincere" (HCSB). The word points to a life free from competing desires.

I can relate to those competing desires. I enjoy the dual hobbies of running and writing. I find both to be fulfilling and both fit in as tools used to live out God's call on my life as a follower of Jesus, but I have discovered that they sometimes conflict—they create World War III nuclear battles in my heart. For example, when I wrote this chapter, I was in the heart of a 14-week marathon training program. I disciplined myself to complete the program in order to improve over last year's time. As a result, I needed and wanted to run because I don't want to get behind on a plan that seems to be working. I wanted to be prepared for a race I had chosen to run.

At the same time I needed and wanted to write this material. I love to write. It is part of God's call on my life to "equip people to know, share, and multiply Christ." Writing exposes my heart to the things of God and is a way for me to share the

> Picture purity as something unmixed, uncompromised, unsullied.

Word of God with others. Sitting down at my computer with a freshly brewed cup of coffee on a crisp fall day is my idea of bliss! I long for the quiet moments filled with the sound of tapping keys and a flow of ideas. For me, writing is invigorating and purposeful. Like running, however, writing is a discipline required to finish a manuscript. Writing demands time, and the time I devote to it cannot be given to another passion or responsibility. So just that morning, I was torn between two passions: one physical, one creative. How do I choose between the two *and* at the same time not neglect my church or my family?

You may have *dueling passions* in your life, too. Beyond those, you undoubtedly have dueling responsibilities. And, whether your passions bring you exhilarating personal fulfillment or your responsibilities are as significant as raising a child, running a department, or charitable service, it is imperative that you not lose focus on the one thing—*one thing!*—you are called to do as a believer in Christ: *pursue unflinching devotion to Him through singleness and purity of heart.* It is no coincidence that the "pure" referred to in Matthew 5:8 means *clean, as in washed.* I believe, with all my faltering and sometimes ill-focused heart, that just as Jesus cleansed us from sin with His death, He also meant for each of us to be cleansed of any distraction that keeps us from the goal of the pursuit of a pure heart.

The People

Picture the word *purity* as something unmixed, uncompromised, unsullied. If something is truly *pure*, it is 100 percent what it says it is—nothing else. There are no additives, no fillers, or no components that compromise or alter it from being 100 percent of what it claims to be. Think of this in terms of everyday items like food and clothing. If a meal is made up of 100 percent pure ingredients, that means it contains no artificial flavorings, colorings, or preservatives. Organic *anything*, free-range *everything*, and certified *whatever* always carries a significantly higher price tag than the preserved-into-the-next-century, processed, petrified, and pre-measured boxes most of us consume on a regular basis. Clearly, pure food is premium food.

Wouldn't it follow then, that if purity of food is considered a premium, how much more so are those "pure in heart" to be valued? Jesus knew the rarity of such sold-out souls, and He blessed them. He knew the tremendous impact people with unmixed motives could have on His kingdom. He saw in such people a straightforwardness that would make them great disciples. He saw passion focused on a single cause: *following Him*. He called these people happy because they knew their "one thing" and were committed to sticking to it no matter what others said. In return for such all-out obedience, Christ promised them the greatest reward imaginable: *to see God*.

PURITY OF HEART OR NAÏVETÉ?

Like the meek and merciful, people without a kingdom view frequently see the pure in heart as either naïve or so narrow-minded that they are ill fit for normal society. In a world of no-holds-barred acceptance, steadfastness to a single view or belief may come across as intolerant, prejudiced or, worse, ignorant. But, Jesus values people who have a single focus and pure motives.

A STRAIGHT-SHOOTING FOLLOWER OF JESUS

As an illustration of what Jesus truly required to be called a disciple, read the following passage from the Book of John (1:43–51):

> *The next day Jesus decided to leave for Galilee. Finding Philip, he said to him, "Follow me."*
>
> *Philip, like Andrew and Peter, was from the town of Bethsaida. Philip found Nathanael and told him, "We have found the one Moses wrote about in the Law, and about whom the prophets also wrote—Jesus of Nazareth, the son of Joseph."*
>
> *"Nazareth! Can anything good come from there?" Nathanael asked.*
>
> *"Come and see," said Philip.*
>
> *When Jesus saw Nathanael approaching, he said of him, "Here is a true Israelite, in whom there is nothing false."*
>
> *"How do you know me?" Nathanael asked.*
>
> *Jesus answered, "I saw you while you were still under the fig tree before Philip called you."*
>
> *Then Nathanael declared, "Rabbi, you are the Son of God; you are the King of Israel."*
>
> *Jesus said, "You believe because I told you I saw you under the fig tree. You shall see greater things than that." He then added, "I tell you the truth, you shall see heaven open, and the angels of God ascending and descending on the Son of Man."*

Did you see that Jesus called Philip first? Philip was compelled to go to Nathanael and bring him to Jesus. Nathanael, however, was clearly underwhelmed at the prospect of meeting Jesus.

> Nathanael was exhibit A for "walking the talk"

Not only did Nathanael *not* openly embrace and honor Jesus, he blatantly dissed his hometown! (v. 46). Like many of his time, Nathanael held preconceived notions about what constituted a proper arrival for the Messiah. It's a safe assumption that he probably envisioned a bit more fanfare for the Savior of the world than a friend-of-a-friend hailing from Nazareth, the hick town far from God's country, Judah.

Nevertheless, Nathanael followed Philip to meet Jesus. When Jesus saw Nathanael approaching, He knew what Nathanael had said about him, but appreciated the man's straightforward way of speaking. Jesus knew that single-minded people make good disciples if they are headed in the right direction. Jesus saw in Nathanael a man who spoke his mind, even if it was potentially offensive. He was a man who stood firmly for integrity and demanded the same of others, just as Jesus did. And just like Jesus, Nathanael spoke straight from his heart. With such gut-level honesty and unwavering commitment to the truth, Jesus knew Nathanael would make an excellent disciple if he would make Jesus Lord of his life. Nathanael did, and Jesus was right.

Nathanael was exhibit A for "walking the talk" of speaking the truth no matter the circumstances or the consequences. He was precisely what Jesus was looking for in people to follow Him. He wanted to reward those pure in heart, free of deceit, single-minded, and intensely focused on following Him with His blessings because He knew it was folks such as these who would speak boldly, live honorably, and make a truly significant difference in people's lives.

The Characteristic

When you first read "the pure in heart . . . will see God" (Matthew 5:8), you most likely thought of purity in the moral sense.

Maybe you thought of the guy on the city bus who's always the first to give up his seat to a female passenger.

Maybe you saw the little old lady down the street who randomly delivers warm cookies to her neighbors' doorsteps as her own sweetshop ministry.

Or, maybe you envisioned purity of heart as your always curious, always observant five-year-old who shadows your every move and thinks you can do no wrong because he loves you so much.

In each case, you would be correct, and you would be thinking biblically. When our motives and intentions line up with what we say and what we do, then we experience purity of heart. Gary and Cathy Deddo of the online Trinity Study Center make a great case for what distinguishes those pure of heart and those consumed with worldly concerns:

> "The pure in heart . . . long to have their inner life and their outer life be the same. They want God in every part of their lives and they look forward to the time where there is no slippage between their outward behavior and their inward character. It will be wonderful, they think, when there is nothing left to hide inside, no dark or shameful secret left."[1]

Did you catch the term "no slippage"? To me that means there is literally no difference between what we value on the inside and how we act on the outside. They are one and the same.

No slippage means our hands become an extension of our heart; our words are the source for filling others' hearts, and our thoughts are focused upon glorifying God in everything in our lives.

> Pure in heart means single in purpose, clean from deceit, and pure in motives

This call to purity of heart isn't just something Jesus mentioned once and moved on. The Bible is full of exhortations and admonitions to constantly work toward becoming pure in heart in order to have the blessing of seeing God. Here are just a few examples:

- David reminded us in Psalm 24 that "he who has clean hands and a pure heart" will ascend the hill of the Lord and stand in God's holy place (Psalm 24:3–4).
- The writer to the Hebrews echoed the words of both Jewish kings (David and Jesus) when he wrote, "Make every effort to live in peace with all men and to be bold; without holiness no one will see the Lord" (Hebrews 12:14).
- James called all Christians to "wash your hands, you sinners, and purify your hearts, you double-minded" (James 4:8).
- Peter called upon his readers, "Now that you have purified yourselves by obeying the truth so that you have sincere love for each other, love one another deeply, from the heart" (1 Peter 1:22 TNIV).

Each of these writers knew that moral purity stems from the heart and is critical to maintaining a right relationship with God. They knew that becoming pure in heart was a constant challenge, to be acknowledged and dealt with every day in hopes of victory or discounted and ignored in admission to defeat.

HYPOCRISY IS THE OPPOSITE OF PURE IN HEART

We get our English word *catharsis* from the Greek word for *pure*. It simply means "cleansed." *Cathartic* means "healing or therapeutic" as in an emotionally explosive moment in the therapy journey when the patient seizes on a core cause of his or her struggles. In the ancient world, to become pure meant to make an object clean from physical stains or dirt. It also meant to become free from sins and faults. A pure heart, then, was a heart free from sin and the duplicity of feeding faults while appearing to live sinless. To be pure in heart was to be single in purpose, clean from deceit, and pure in motives. Persons who were pure in heart were not hypocrites living a double standard; how they appeared on the outside was how they genuinely were on the inside.

Hypocrites, however, were just the opposite. Their seemingly faultless lifestyle was nothing more than a charade meant to give others the impression that their every thought, word, and action was done in obedience. They were obedient, all right—just obedient to the wrong thing. Religious leaders in Jesus' day, for example, chose honoring the law to the tiniest detail while neglecting "justice, mercy and faithfulness" (Matthew 23:23). In direct defiance to Jesus' teachings, their inner motives bore no resemblance to their outwardly pious behavior.

Because of this, Jesus hated the disease of hypocrisy that plagued God's people and destroyed their relationship with God and others. He attacked it at every turn. In the last week of His ministry on earth, Jesus confronted the religious

We are created to serve only one Master.

leaders who practiced and enforced the most outrageously hypocritical lifestyles.

Jesus detested duplicity of any sort. Whether it was a double standard for the social classes or inconsistencies between a person's actions and their words, Jesus instituted the first zero tolerance policy among those who would be His followers. It was literally "His way or the highway." The only caveat, however, was that "the highway" led defectors straight to the pit of hell.

THE SECRET TO HOW YOU ARE MADE

Jesus provided a secret about how we are designed as human beings. The Creator cracked open the manual of our existence and revealed in very clear language how He wired us. To reveal this secret, Jesus placed the love of wealth as a rival god to the one true God. His unequivocal perspective is clear in the following saying:

> *No one can serve two masters. Either he will hate the one and love the other, or he will be devoted to the one and despise the other. You cannot serve both God and Money.*
>
> — MATTHEW 6:24

There it is again—that pesky demand for purity of heart and the lack of tolerance to share a believer's loyalty with another competing (little *g*) god or detractor. Jesus knew it was impossible to serve two masters. It is inevitable that one will win out over the other and we'll neglect, if not grow to resent, the other. God created us with a heart that beats for only one ultimate loyalty.

Jesus taught this fundamental truth of life: we are created to serve only one Master.

In everyday terms, that means you likely cannot be an Olympic marathoner and a Pulitzer Prize–winning writer—at least in the same year! To be so totally sold out to absolute excellence in one of these areas necessarily means the sacrifice of excellence (maybe even proficiency!) in the other. We end up being a "Jack-of-all-trades, master of none," according to the English adage. This is true in our spiritual lives too. And it works the same way when our human, usually self-centered, desires come up against all-out submission to Christ. We simply cannot serve God wholeheartedly and satisfy all our other earthly desires.

PURITY OF HEART AS IT AFFECTS OTHERS

Purity of heart is essential for authentic relationships with others to thrive and strengthen over time. Trust, transparency, and a sense of community are all built upon honesty, openness, and vulnerability with others. A mind and heart mired in ulterior motives and self-serving rewards cannot consistently invest in others without betraying confidences, breaking bonds, and ruining relationships. A cleansed heart, not one covered in selfishness and deceit, is the necessary basis for relationships that foster the peace of God. Remember that we've reached the summit of this journey where we began to hunger and thirst for the things of God. It is now our responsibility to return to the valley of our relationships to bring to them the peace of God. There is no room for hypocrisy in these revisited relationships; deceit never builds trust within a community. Our hearts are changed as a result of reaching the summit and embracing God's righteousness. From that banquet table of forgiveness and renewal, we descend to rebuild our relationships with others by showing mercy and being authentic, both of which flow from a purified heart.

The Promise

Jesus promised that those with a pure heart would "see God." That's an awesome promise! He didn't say we *might* snag a glance of God. Or *hopefully* we would see God. Neither did He dangle some enticing phrase such as *highly probable* regarding our chances of seeing God if we were to become pure in heart. He clearly and emphatically made the connection between possessing a pure heart and seeing God without additional conditions.

Hallelujah! Sound the bells! Shout "Amen" from the rooftops!

And yet . . .

And yet the Bible teaches that no one can see God and live to tell about it (Exodus 33:20). It also makes it clear that "without holiness no one will see the Lord" (Hebrews 12:14).

So which way is it? Should we believe one Scripture passage and not another? Do we righteously pursue a heart that's pure, claiming Christ's promise in the Beatitudes or do we accept the impossibility of ever seeing God and abandon all efforts toward that end? Doesn't it have to be one way or the other?

I believe there are at least three suitable answers to our dilemma:

THE PURE IN HEART WILL SEE JESUS HIMSELF

The pure in heart would "see God" in the person of Jesus. As in other Beatitudes, Jesus revealed who He was as the Sent One of God through His blessings and promises. I base this explanation upon John 1:18: “No one has ever seen God. The only Son—the One who is at the Father’s side—He has revealed Him” (John 1:18 HCSB).

We get our English word *exegesis* from the word that means “the explanation or critical analysis of a word or passage that leads you to its true meaning.” A literal translation of John 1:18 would read, “No one has ever seen God, but Jesus, who is at the Father’s side, is the exegesis of God.” The verse teaches that knowing Jesus is to know and understand God. The physical Jesus “interprets” the invisible, Triune God.

THE PURE IN HEART WILL SEE THE WAYS OF GOD

When your heart and mind have been cleansed by God’s mercy, you can understand the ways of God. Read this passage from Paul’s letter to the Romans and pay particular attention to the cause-and-effect relationship between experiencing mercy and understanding God:

> *Therefore, I urge you, brothers, in view of God’s mercy, to offer your bodies as living sacrifices, holy and pleasing to God—this is your spiritual act of worship. Do not conform any longer to the pattern of this world, but be transformed by the renewing of your mind. Then you will be able to test and approve what God’s will is—his good, pleasing, and perfect will.*
>
> —Romans 12:1–2

This version of Scripture tells us we will “be able to test and approve” God’s will; another version says we will be able to “discern” (HCSB) His will; and still a third translation grants that we will be able to "prove" (NKJV) God's will. Although He phrased it slightly differently in the Beatitudes, Jesus made this very same promise. He told us if God transforms our heart, we will be able to discern God's will or see the ways of God.

THE PURE IN HEART WILL SEE GOD'S WORK IN OTHERS

When we maintain pure motives, we are frequently allowed to see what is genuinely happening in other people's lives. As mercy supplies empathy for the condition of others, purity of heart frees us to serve them in their time of need. If we harbor a deceitful heart, we're more inclined to take advantage of shared confidences and known weaknesses, but a pure heart drives us to meet the needs of others sincerely and with their best interest at heart, not ours. A pure heart also ascribes pure motives to the actions of others. When we are acting selflessly toward others, we more easily believe others are acting the same way. When we possess a wicked heart, we are decidedly quicker to assume the same in others.

If we stay mindful of Christ's grace and mercy in our own lives and filter all calls to judgment of others through these humble lenses, our chances of becoming pure in heart are increased exponentially.

The Illness

Most people want good relationships with others *and* a good reputation. That desire creates the danger of paying more attention to our behavior than to our heart. It's like looking good in the ski lodge but never going on the slopes, or, wearing all the tennis fashions and never playing a game. This look-like-but-never-play behavior, in turn, affects the motives behind our actions. In many cases, it is easier to keep clean the things other people see and neglect the things that only God can see. *Character is a matter of the heart*. It is the quality of our intimate fellowship with God.[2] If our hearts harbor darkness, we may be able to hide that darkness by religious behavior. But crisis and leisure expose true character, and no matter the quality of your playacting, who you are in your heart will show itself in your actions.

A deceitful heart always leads to a dishonest portrayal of who we are.

The illness of a pure heart is trying to manufacture such a heart with our efforts and outward behavior rather than trusting Jesus for the cleansing and renewing of our hearts. We may be among the first to arrive and the last to leave our church's Sunday morning service, but if that is the only time we visit with God each week, then our spiritual self is severely malnourished and we're nowhere near the spiritual pillar we appear to be. We become like the Pharisees rather than the humble disciples of Jesus.

In another way, we can dress in the finest clothes head to toe, but if we don't honor the body we hang them on, it is all for naught. Tight jeans expose your love for sweets, not hide it! If you spend all your time working on your behavior to appear to be a follower of Jesus, you are in the trap of the Pharisees—experts at playacting and complete failures at character. When challenged by Jesus about serving money rather than God, for example, Luke tells us, "The Pharisees, who loved money, heard all this and were sneering at Jesus" (Luke 16:14). And Jesus, knowing their character, said to them, "You are the ones who justify yourselves in the eyes of men, but God knows your hearts. What is highly valued among men is detestable in God's sight" (Luke 16:15). *God knows your heart!* This truth is why the spiritual illness of playacting always ends in exposure.

Keep in mind that the opposite of a pure heart is not some specific sinful act. The opposite of a pure heart is a deceitful heart, and a deceitful heart always leads to a dishonest portrayal of who we are. There was a reason Jesus gave much of His attention in the Sermon on the Mount to the vast chasm between authentic discipleship and religious activity. He knew the captivating hold a belief in following the rules and abiding solely by the letter of the law could have on us and He wanted more for us. He wanted our sights set on Him and the commitment to live for His glory.

The Exercise

The spiritual exercise that sustains a pure heart cleansed by the Lord and singleness of motive is *fasting*. Our hearts must constantly be tested and refined to remove the sin of deceit and to restore purity of motives. A pure heart is a constant concern, not a final reality—at least not until we are made whole in eternity.

TYPES OF FASTING

Fasting is more than going for a time without eating. Fasting is designed to discipline the physical in order to nurture the spiritual. By removing something worldly and replacing it with something spiritual, we move toward spiritual wellness. We can fast from anything that takes our attention away from God. The list of people, places, and things that compete for our attention is literally endless. Here are a few suggestions of fasting options:

- Consider fasting from feeding your information habit for one week. Pray that God would show you real needs and issues in your community and world through talking to others. Rather than reading your chosen blogs, news feeds, or following others on Twitter, pray for ways God can use you to bring peace and justice into those circumstances you know about firsthand through others.
- Fast from email for a day. Use the telephone or conversations for all of your contacts. This is a way to restore the priority of relationships in your life.
- Turn off the television for an evening and use that time for Bible study and prayer. Replace entertainment with *inner-attainment.*

- Replace your radio shows with praise and worship CDs or podcasts of Christian leaders during your daily commute time. Doing so will allow your mind to be renewed by the things of God.
- Skip one meal one day. Use that time to pray for Christian brothers and sisters around the world who are suffering persecution because of their beliefs. Take the money you would have spent on those meals and give it to your church or an organization serving such people.

PRINCIPLES OF FASTING

Fasting must be God-centered.

Jesus warned His followers to be careful not to bring attention to themselves when they fasted, but to do so rather as an exercise of the heart (Matthew 6:16–18). We cannot bribe or control God through fasting, and we must not use it to honor ourselves by looking religious. The focus of fasting should always be on our relationship with God. Tony Jones reminds us, "Fasting is a spiritual remedy to what is, really, a spiritual problem. To fast shows our reliance upon God for all things. It reminds us that we are, ultimately, spiritual beings. It confirms that 'man does not live by bread alone.'"[3]

Fasting endurance must be built slowly.

Like any discipline, when you fast, you must begin slowly and gradually increase your intensity or difficulty level. Just as you wouldn't set out to run ten miles the day after you buy new running shoes and a running outfit, your first fast shouldn't be a wilderness 40 days and nights fast either. Honorable efforts and consistent increases in our fasting intensity and duration will gradually bring about what God desires most from us: a deepened dependence on and a strengthened relationship with Him.

Fasting from food must focus on appetite for God.

Not eating for a time is the simplest and most time-honored way to fast. Fasting from food replaces physical sustenance with spiritual nutrition. Jesus said to His disciples once when they asked Him if He were hungry, "My food is to do the will of him who sent me and to finish his work" (John 4:34). Jesus fed on obedience to the will of the Father. To Him, physical food was a distant second.

As a food fast disciplines your appetite for food so your appetite for God can increase, to tame your appetite for food is to tame your other appetites. As your desire for food grows, fill it with time spent with God. If you sense God leading you to fast, eat a light lunch that excludes caffeine and sugar. Refrain from eating an evening meal. The next morning, go directly to a time of Bible study and prayer. After a time with God, break your fast with light cereals and fruit. If you sense God would have you continue the fast, extend it until noon and break it at the noon meal. Whenever you end it, don't stuff yourself in order to compensate for your hunger.

A God-ordained fast allows for God to renew and purify your heart. The exercise allows the Holy Spirit to reveal the deceit that keeps you from loving God with all your heart, soul, mind and strength. Pray God will lead you to this intimate time with Him so that your love for Him will continue to grow.

Takeaway

A pure heart is God's way of preparing us for authentic relationships with Him and others. As we've done in previous chapters, let's review the path we have climbed to reach this point. Our poverty of soul leads us to mourn; grief over our sin then leads to repentance. A changed heart brings us to meekness and a fresh encounter with God. Through our God-given meekness, we begin to hunger and thirst after God, and, as we are filled through the Holy Spirit's presence in our lives, we are then directed back to the valley of relationships as a changed person. From a mountaintop mercy-filled experience with God, we begin to show God's mercy to others. A pure heart is the way station for the spiritual traveler that promises to see God, His ways, and His work in the life of others. The exercise of fasting offers periods of reflection and cleansing by God to keep our hearts and motives pure toward God and others.

Questions for Reflection

1. What were your first impressions of Jesus' blessing toward the pure in heart? Who have you known that you could describe in this way?

2. How would you describe hypocrisy? Where have you seen it in others? Where have you seen it in your behavior?

3. What are some ways you have "seen God" as promised by Jesus in this beatitude? Write an example or two here.

4. Have you ever practiced the spiritual discipline of fasting? If so, when was the last time? What did God reveal to you during that time? If you have never fasted, seek God's leadership in trying this practice.

CHAPTER 9

The Peacemakers

Blessed are the peacemakers, for they will be called sons of God.

—MATTHEW 5:9

Jessica parked her car in a distant spot outside one of the hotels near the bustling airport. It wasn't the nicest overnight housing, but it wasn't the seediest either. It was the kind that catered to small businesses that didn't have the luxury of an open-ended expense account. And, it was the last place on earth she wanted to be right now.

She had followed her husband from their home across town. Within minutes of pulling into the parking lot every fear and suspicion of the last six months was confirmed as she watched her husband of 12 years walk into the hotel with another woman. In an instant, she knew her life would change inalterably; regardless of what she did, what she said, what he did, and what he said—life for her would always be viewed as "before" and "after" her discovery.

As the evening grew dark around her, she knew she had a choice to make. Should she confront him and risk the wrath of his violent temper? For years, she had avoided conflict whenever possible to keep the peace in their relationship. Sure, she had her own opinions, preferences, and wishes, but in the end, it was always easier to keep them to herself and keep the peace between them. The fallout just wasn't worth speaking up.

She considered the possible outcomes if she decided to confront him. Anger? Shame? Even desperate excuses? She couldn't be sure. One thing she was sure of though: a voice that spoke straight to her heart and said, "Go to him. I'll be there with you." And with that, she opened the car door.

Avoiding eye contact with anyone in the hotel lobby, she walked straight to the front desk where she signed in as her husband's wife. Though he had registered as a single, hotel personnel knew far better than to question their guests' marital status. The clerk handed her the room key and pointed her to the ground floor elevators.

Jessica pressed the button for the correct floor as the elevator doors closed. When they opened, she took a deep breath and braced for the biggest confrontation of her life, armed with little more than the still, small voice that had urged her forward. While I won't give you the rest of the details, I will tell you Jessica confronted her husband and stood strong in the Lord through the weeks and months that followed that courageous moment.

I changed some of the details (including her real name) in Jessica's story, but it is based on true events I encounter all too often. Her story illustrates the painful and difficult steps it sometimes takes to bring peace to a broken relationship. Before peace can reign, people must face the sometimes-difficult, sometimes-sobering, and sometimes-painful truth about realities in their lives. Reconciliation doesn't stand a chance of happening without repentance, and repentance doesn't happen without exposing sin *and* embracing truth.

When I consider the courage it took to confront her husband with another woman at the hotel that night, I'm not so sure I would have had the same conviction to follow through as Jessica did. For me, the absence of conflict ranks very near the top of the list of my emotional needs. I want peace in and around my family, at my church, and among my closest circle of friends. Sometimes, however, that means I must be willing to pay the price of truthful confrontation and careful restoration.

Jesus blessed those who would be peacemakers because He knew that orchestrating peace was rarely an easy, heartwarming experience—at least at first. He knew what it meant to deal with headstrong, my-way-or-the-highway type A people literally hell-bent on honoring themselves above the Savior. He knew that it was the go-between, or the mediator, who often got the worst end of the deal when it came to brokering peace between fractured parties. And He knew that, short of a calling or Spirit-breathed conviction from Christ, most people would rather do just about anything than serve as a peacemaker. That is precisely why He chose to honor these few-and-far-between brave souls and claim them as "sons of God" (v. 9).

The People

Jesus initially blessed those in the crowd who were potentially people of His kingdom. He then blessed those who had or would become His peacemakers. That left a lot of people still in limbo: they hadn't received His lifesaving blessing but they also didn't know which way to turn. They were caught somewhere between those wanting and needing Christ and those in total denial of His eternal gift. Such lukewarm indecisiveness was a no-man's-land as far as Christ was concerned. In the end, there were two primary groups that Jesus intentionally did *not* bless: the peace*keepers* and those who saw peace merely as *an absence of conflict*. Let's look closer at each group.

JESUS DID NOT BLESS PEACE*KEEPERS*

Peacekeepers do not do the hard work of creating peace; they merely work to keep things the way they are without doing the heavy lifting of actually creating peace where there is none. For example, the United States armed forces enter a conflict to establish peace, while NATO troops are sent in to maintain that peace. In the opening story of Jessica, a peacekeeper might have swallowed the hurt and pain and returned home to live as a victim in a broken marriage. Peacemakers face the tough job of hammering out peace, whether it happens on the battlefield, in palace halls or in a betrayed relationship. As a result of this often unpopular, and always trying, job description, Jesus deliberately blessed people who were bold enough to face problems and to negotiate peace with justice.

JESUS DID NOT BLESS THOSE WHO SEE PEACE AS SIMPLY A LACK OF CONFLICT

Peace always comes at a price. Sometimes it costs actual dollars between conflicting parties. Sometimes it costs someone's pride. Sometimes peace only comes at concession by a person or peoples, and sometimes peace demands the lives of brave servicemen and women on foreign soil. Eternal peace for you, me, and all who would follow Him, required Jesus to give up His life at the hands of unbelieving and self-protective religious leaders (Ephesians 2:14–15).

Genuine peace exists between two parties when the core issues of conflict have been resolved. Peace comes as a result of reconciliation. Living in the absence of conflict does not mean that true peace is present. For any depth of relational significance to take place, you have to get beyond the niceties of life—in long-standing friendships, in marriage, and especially in a soul-saving relationship with Christ. *Jesus knew that true transformation that leads to peace inevitably comes with conflict.* Sometimes it's dramatic, traumatic, and gut-wrenching; other times it's a barely audible concession. Whatever the road we each must travel to establish Christ's kingdom within our souls and our relationships with others, the journey demands we confront our old selves and accept and address the aspects of our lives that conflict with Christ's criteria before we become one of His.

True transformation that leads to peace inevitably comes with conflict.

JESUS DID BLESS THOSE WHO GIVE THEIR LIVES FOR PEACE

The peace I'm referring to here is the peace of God and it pertains to *all* of our relationships—the easy ones, the obligatory ones, and the I'll-put-up-with-you-because-you're-my-sister-in-law ones. All of our relationships—not just the ones we deem worthy, mutually beneficial, or honorable deserve to be addressed honestly: A-L-L of them.

Jesus blessed those who stepped into tough situations to wrestle until the peace of God ruled. He knew the war wounds of the afflicted peacemakers: all-consuming sadness, battered emotions, and deep, deep scars left from accusations,

> To have a relationship with Jesus is not always a peaceful decision.

insinuations, and questioned motives—because He experienced them all personally. During His days on earth, Jesus sought out those who bore the bruises from intervening between warring parties. He intentionally searched the many crowds that followed Him, actively seeking out those who were fatigued from working to make peace an option in a world of conflict. He wanted to identify them so He could claim them as His own.

Peacemaking is the sign of transformation in a person's heart. It is a proactive verb that implies intervention and engagement with conflicting parties. Just like the people who were called to be peacemakers during Jesus' time, those called today are most effective when they have thoroughly experienced and solidly embraced each of the traits we have discussed leading up to spiritual wellness to this point. To bypass or discount any of the progressive steps of the Beatitudes is to seriously hinder the impact of the subsequent stages. It's not unlike putting the cart before the horse so to speak—it is taking things out of their spiritually intended order and yet still expecting the same transformative outcome.

The journey of spiritual wellness begins with poverty of spirit and ends with the courage to proactively bring God's peace into every relationship. The focus turns from me to others. The ability to make peace in relationships is the ultimate indication that a person has moved from self-centeredness to other-centeredness. You cannot make peace in relationships if you are trying to protect or build your ego. A narcissist never needs to change, but everyone else does! Peacemaking comes at the end of our descent from the spiritual mountaintop feast into the valley of relationships *because we cannot be peacemakers until God makes peace in our hearts.*

The Characteristic

To be a peacemaker is to be like Jesus. Other than our Rescuer or Savior, I can think of no other word that more accurately describes all that Christ was sent to earth to accomplish. It is one of the most effective ways we can emulate Christ and portray His likeness in us. To bring about peace, to represent peace, and to make peace possible for all that would come after Him was the primary reason Christ walked among us.

Many knew Jesus as the Prince of Peace, including the prophet Isaiah (Isaiah 9:6). At His birth, the angels announced that He would bring "peace to men on whom his favor rests" (Luke 2:14). The comfort He offered His disciples was peace-centered: "Peace I leave with you; my peace I give you. I do not give to you as the world gives. Do not let your hearts be troubled and do not be afraid" (John 14:27). Paul knew firsthand that Jesus brought peace to those He loved. Paul taught that Jesus "is our peace, who has made the two one and has destroyed the barrier, the dividing wall of hostility" as he wrote to Jewish and non-Jewish Christians (Ephesians 2:14). Jesus is God's Son and He was sent to bring peace to *all* people and *all* relationships.

A DIFFERENT KIND OF PEACE

I think it is extremely important to note that the peace Christ brought is not what we always associate with peace. Whereas we might characterize it as meaning an evening without a fight over the remote or a family reunion without any punches thrown, Jesus described His peace differently than the world's standards. He elaborated on what this meant when He said,

> *Do not suppose that I have come to bring peace to the earth. I did not come to bring peace, but a sword. For I have come to turn a man against his father, a daughter against her mother, a daughter-in-law against her mother-in-law—a man's enemies will be the members of his own household. Anyone who loves his father or mother more than me is not worthy of me; anyone who loves his son or daughter more than me is not worthy of me; and anyone who does not take his cross and follow me is not worthy of me. Whoever finds his life will lose it, and whoever loses his life for my sake will find it.*
>
> —MATTHEW 10:34–39

To have a relationship with Jesus is not always a peaceful decision. The choice to follow Jesus causes conflicts between earthly relationships and kingdom goals—with others and within us. This is true for *everyone* who follows Christ for any substantial amount of time. If it hasn't happened to you yet, it will, and you should be prepared for it when it does.

Maybe you were raised in a Christian home and came to trust Christ at an early age—congratulations; your early years were possibly uneventful, spiritually speaking. But give it a few years, bring a few "outsiders" into the family fold, and all of a sudden, not everyone sees things exactly how you've been taught.

Say your sister is totally and completely swept off her feet by a man who considers each of us to be "our own religion." And while his claim smacks of why-can't-we-all-just-live-and-let-live inclusiveness, your sister can't see past the stars in her eyes. Ask yourself what happens when Easter comes around and your soon-to-be brother-in-law disses discussions of the Resurrection and explains it away as little more than folklore. Peaceful Easter brunch at Grandma's? Probably not.

What if you're the "token Christian" in your group of friends? You know how it goes—they think you're the "nice" one, the Goody Two-shoes of the group, the one whose moral compass consistently points north. You good-naturedly accept the friendly kidding and don't call anyone out for their occasional dip in integrity until . . . until one of the girls of the group announces she's pregnant and not intending to keep the baby. The timing is simply "not right" she explains. There's grad school still to finish, money is tight, and besides, the father doesn't want anything more to do with her. Immediately she garners the sympathy of the group when she shares her news—she certainly wouldn't want the responsibility at this point in her life, and the girls can completely identify with the overwhelming responsibility it would be to raise a child alone. In the time it takes to move from appetizers to main course, this unwanted pregnancy is presented and resolved as "a major inconvenience" by some of your closest friends. Do you broach the life-and-death gravity of this conversation and risk the "c'mon, man, you're-soooo-outta-touch"

The peace that transforms lives sometimes feels like anything but peace.

judgment of your friends or dodge the dilemma and ask the waitress for some extra catsup?

See what I mean? This peacemaking mission usually is filled with consequences—hurtful, unkind, and judgmental consequences. *The peace that transforms lives sometimes feels like anything but peace.* Jesus warned that making peace would sometimes involve conflict. In fact, the spiritual peace that results from our relationship with Jesus forms the basis of being a peacemaker. We cannot be peacemakers until we have experienced peace in our relationship with God. That would be like trying to teach someone how to ride a bike when you had never even gotten up on two wheels. Fortunately, Christ makes gracious provisions for His followers and amply equips us before calling us into service. Enter the empowering Holy

Spirit, who brings peace to Jesus' followers and enables them to put on spiritual armor and act as peacemakers.

Proactive peacemaking is a hallmark of a Christian. In fact, it is one of the hallmarks of distinction between Christianity and other religions. Jesus insisted that His followers not resist but love their enemies—and in doing so, He offered them the peace of God and the "ministry of reconciliation" (2 Corinthians 5:17–19). Jesus knew His followers would make peace by bringing the reconciling work of Christ into the lives of those they touched.

The Promise

Jesus said the peacemakers would gain a reputation. He said they would be "called sons of God" (Matthew 5:9), and He promised those who brought the peace of God into relationships would be called the "children of God" (TNIV). He reinforced this beatitude when He taught, "But I tell you: Love your enemies and pray for those who persecute you, that you may be sons of your Father in heaven" (Matthew 5:44-45). Jesus promised His followers would gain a reputation for being God's children if they became His peacemakers.

I can't think of another reputation that I would be more honored to carry. Sure, I want to be known as a loving husband, caring dad, and great grandpa. And yeah, I certainly hope my church members consider me a worthy shepherd to guide them into greatness in their walk with Christ. Heck, I'd even like to be known in my running circles as a mentor, trainer, and positive example of a physically fit, aging man. But if all these titles by association were to disappear and I was left only with my reputation as a child of God that would be sufficient. Don't misread that—I'm not wishing any of these relationships away (especially the ones involving my grandchildren!). I'm just far enough down this life journey to see and value the supreme importance of being recognized as a child of God.

CHILDREN OF GOD

Imagine what would happen if a group as small as a neighborhood embraced this often-unpopular challenge to love our enemies. Maybe the families with diametrically opposing political yard signs could see past the personalities of the candidates to the real issues that impact them. Or, instead of grumbling about the overgrown state of the foreclosed home on the corner, maybe a few teenagers could come together and stage their own "extreme yard makeover" for everyone's benefit. Or, maybe instead of living in fear and suspicion, neighbors could come together and form a crime watch patrol. Imagine the tremendous example this would set for nearby neighborhoods and subdivisions; and these aren't people engaged in serious conflict!

What if you ramped up the neighborhood discord several levels where neighbor fought against neighbor on everything from property lines to noise levels? What if, at the height of all the hoopla, with fingers pointing, voices rising, and threats elevating, one of the neighbors simply stepped back from the conflict and dialed the dissension down a notch. Or 2. Or 12. He sees the opportunity to step in as a peacemaker and seizes it.

If we consistently treat our enemies as Jesus commanded, wouldn't others eventually notice something different? I think they would. I believe we would develop a reputation—a good, honorable reputation, if we chose to love our enemies in the name of Jesus rather than slugging it out with them.

Gaining a reputation as being a child of God can be an awesome thing. Recall that since God has begun to develop authentic meekness in our lives, we don't allow what others think of us to puff us up or inflate our self-ego. Rather our response to other's recognition of us as "sons of God" should only cause us to praise the One who waged the peace in our own lives. Keep in mind our journey to this point has been a transformation—first from attention to self, to worship of God, and ultimately to service to others in the name of Jesus. At this point, our motives are to be pure, relying on the mercy of God to help us bring peace to others. The long and the short of it: acting and acquiring a reputation as a child of God should add to our humility, not boost our pride—because that has already found its proper place on our journey to God's mercy.

Take heed that Jesus' promise is also a warning: having a reputation as a child of God brings persecution from those who oppose God. We'll address this more in the final chapter, but understand that Jesus was brutally honest in His promise: *peacemakers who gain a reputation of acting like God will bring opposition on themselves*. This isn't meant to cause you fear, just to forewarn you. And as an encouragement, it helps to remember that you're in good company when you are persecuted. People treated the prophets and Jesus the same way. Those who rejected the peace Jesus came to offer them crucified the Prince of Peace.

Personally benefiting or getting our way is not making peace.

The Illness

The spiritual illness of distorted peacemaking can appear in three ways: the absence of conflict as the primary goal of your actions, forcing a peace without the love of God as your motive, and making peace "your way or the highway."

THE ABSENCE OF CONFLICT AS A GOAL

Remember that we previously established that this perception of peace is incorrect: the absence of conflict. Those who buy into this misconception may believe that working to keep others from fighting is akin to acceptable peacemaking. In these instances, *personal comfort becomes the goal*, not renewing damaged relationships.

The mother who separates her quarreling children from one another all day long may bring herself some momentary peace, but she has done little to teach her children how to get along with each other well. Likewise, the domineering father who uses intimidation and threats to keep the house quiet during game time may have a silence for a few hours, but he's way off base in terms of cultivating genuine peace within his home's four walls. Just because peacemaking within relationships sometimes brings conflict with it doesn't mean that it shouldn't be pursued. If the confrontation or disagreement result in healthier and more authentic relationships, the discomfort is worth the temporary tension.

FORCING PEACE WITHOUT THE LOVE OF GOD

A second illness or misdirection of peacemaking is to force peace into a situation without the love of God as your motive. Orchestrating events or brokering peace for benefits beyond the relationship are not actions that bring glory to Jesus, and yet people do it all the time for personal benefit. Not only is Christ dishonored, but the integrity of the collaborator is cheapened. The Jackson family was one such case. They had been in the oil business for three generations, but when one of the grown sons wanted to go into another line of business, he hurt feelings and caused others to question his loyalty to the family. The relationship between father and son was severely damaged when the youngest, Andy, struck out on his own and went to work in the city.

When oil spiked to a near-record high, Andy's young wife started making casual comments about "the importance of family" and how "happy Dad would be if you just gave him a call." It seemed like an admirable concern at first until Andy's new bride revealed her true motives in a heated exchange one day.

"I can't believe you are walking away from the *gold mine* in your dad's business," she yelled. "Do you realize what kind of a life we could have with that kind of money? And you . . . you're just content to let your brothers have it all! Can't you just swallow your pride and tell them you want back in?"

So much for the young lady's concern for renewed family relations. Sounds like her case of extreme "poor, poor me" cost her more than some new dining room furniture; it cost her a serious hit to her character as well as the disappointment of Christ.

In contrast, the peacemakers Jesus blessed are those who are motivated by God's love and mercy. For us, that means that we want to bring peace into the lives of others because God has changed *our* hearts. *Personally benefiting or getting our way is not making peace.* Pursuing outside gain or stroking our ego can never be a part of this characteristic of spiritual wellness. Position, power, or authority should never be a part of the process to change hearts. Genuine peace only comes from God's merciful work in a life. We are merely instruments of God's peace, *not* the power behind it.

MAKING PEACE OUR WAY WILL FAIL

A third improper type of peacemaking seeks to use only the ways of human reason to accomplish the ways of God. Social justice without spiritual peace can turn into idolatry if taken to the extreme. Too often we put our hope in peace brought about by laws rather than in the work of God to change hearts. I think of the volatile state of the legislation surrounding abortion as a perfect example of that which cannot be fully addressed through legal rulings. Whether legal or not, the issue must become a matter of the heart if Christ is to be honored. A changed heart rather than a new law should be the first goal of a follower of Jesus.

The Exercise

Spiritual exercises are not exclusive to the development of any one beatitude. Just as physical exercises targeted for your legs can benefit your entire body, single spiritual exercises can enhance every aspect of your life. If you've ever engaged in an exercise or training regimen, you know that the regularity of the discipline works to create a sort of dependence on doing the actual running, strength training, or flexibility exercises. While you may or may not actually enjoy the training, you do enjoy the benefits, and you come to miss them if you skip a day or two. You feel sluggish, all wound up, off your game.

The good news is that this discipline-breeds-dependence in a spiritual sense is easily started or resumed. For me, the whole sold-out, complete and utter dependence on Christ begins and ends with *prayer*—*my* prayers with God. My confessions, my victories, my fears, my desires—my *everything* rises and falls on my prayer life. Prayer should be part of every Christian's life and not just of those who are in the ministry of peacemaking, but prayer is absolutely *essential* to *this* work of God.

Why is prayer so integral to peacemaking? Philip Yancey, reflecting on the power of prayer in the ministry of Bishop Desmond Tutu's peacemaking ministry in South Africa concluded,

> *In prayer we stand before God to plead our condition as well as the conditions around us. In the process, the act of prayer emboldens me to join the work of transforming the world into a place where the Father's will is indeed done as it is in heaven. We are Christ's body on earth, after all; he has no hands but ours.*

> *And yet to act as Christ's body we need an unbroken connection to the Head. We pray in order to see the world with God's eyes, and then to join the stream of power as it breaks loose.*[1]

Prayer changes our hearts so we can bring the peace of God that changes the hearts of others.

PRAYER IS THE LIFELINE FROM THE PEACEMAKER TO THE PEACE GIVER—JESUS

Prayer links us to the peace of God through an ongoing communion with Him. Jesus, who is the Prince of Peace, spent many hours praying to the Father as He completed His mission on earth. If Jesus committed so much time and energy to staying in touch with the Father, seeking His direction, beseeching His will, shouldn't we at least take note and make it a lifelong goal to mirror the same? For me, following Jesus and praying are inextricable. To be a follower of Jesus is to follow Him in prayer.

Prayer is important to peacemaking because it helps us see the "powers" and "principalities" (Ephesians 6:12 KJV) into which we must bring the peace of God. It also helps us see the marketplaces and the cubicles and the Little League games where we are called to bring His peace. We cannot recognize these spiritual opportunities for all their potential without a continual conversation with God. Without prayer our spiritual eyes are not sharp enough to recognize the spiritual forces at work in the relationships needing the peace of God.

Everyday conflicts between friends would be discounted as unreasonable and illogical without prayer. Relationship-ending family feuds would be left to fester without prayer. And, life-giving alliances might never be formed without prayer alerting us to the possibilities.

Prayer allows us to remain filled with God's presence and power. Remember that Jesus promised that if we hunger and thirst for righteousness we would be filled. Just as eating is essential to staying filled with nourishment, so we stay filled with righteousness through prayer. Continued prayer with God will keep our hearts pure and our egos in check so we can join God in the work of peacemaking.

Takeaway

We once again find ourselves in the valley of relationships after having ascended into the presence of God on our spiritual wellness journey. God has prepared us to bring His peace to each relationship of our lives. He has called us to be peacemakers. Just as God has changed your heart, He has changed the hearts of others. Watching the peace of God rule in the hearts of others is the joy of being a peacemaker. Your reputation grows as a child of God. Some will rejoice with you; others will want to be rid of you. This divisive reality is the basis of Jesus' final blessing in the Beatitudes.

Questions for Reflection

1. What emotions did you feel as you read Jessica's story? Have you ever done a similar act to begin the process of making peace in a relationship?

2. Write or discuss how you can apply Jesus' call to be a peacemaker in your relationships? What are some reasons why you may not be obedient to His call?

3. How often do you pray with God about making Christ-centered peace in your home, in your church, in your community, or in your country? Write about one or two issues or relationships God may call you to enter as His peacemaker?

CHAPTER 10

The Persecuted

Blessed are those who are persecuted because of righteousness, for theirs is the kingdom of heaven.

—Matthew 5:10

Rick was a man with a vision—a far-reaching, all-inclusive, gospel-spreading vision. In his role as a leader in an association of churches in a southern state, Rick sensed a call that the member churches needed to better reflect the ethnic makeup of the communities they represented. That meant making a concerted effort to develop churches primarily targeted at attracting new African American members.

He quickly went to work garnering support, collecting resources, and enlisting workers to make his vision a reality. Through his committed leadership, the number of black churches in the association grew from 8 to 18 in only a matter of a few years. An overlooked population was filling a kingdom void as they were welcomed and embraced, and the response from the community was tremendously enthusiastic.

As a result of the solid commitment and ample support the new churches enjoyed, Rick thought the next natural next step was to invite the leaders of these churches to accept leadership roles within the association. In doing so, they would bring a much-needed perspective to the roundtable as the churches served each other and the community. It seemed like a win-win.

Within months of these new members assuming leadership positions, trouble began. On Halloween following their appointments, Rick got a call from another staff member telling him that their offices were up in flames. Three firehouse alarms and thousands of gallons of water later, Rick stood behind the official crime scene yellow tape staring at the smoldering pile of charred plywood, water-saturated ceiling tiles, and broken windows. He was anxious to walk through the remains and salvage anything that hadn't been ruined by fire, smoke, or water, but fire investigators were still making their preliminary assessments. All indications suggested a bomb was the initial cause. Not only was the association's building completely ruined, but the fire was set intentionally—malicious, vengeful, and intended to bring harm.

State and local investigative agencies soon became involved. Not long after the fire, Rick received a threatening letter, decidedly discouraging him from furthering his efforts to grow the African American Christian community's involvement in association affairs. Word got back to him that his picture even showed up on a far-removed church's bulletin board with the caption "The Anti-Christ" written beneath it. Authorities placed a 24-hour guard on Rick and his family.

Everywhere he went, he wondered if someone would try to take his life. The guy hurrying past him on the sidewalk suddenly seemed suspicious. The pizza delivery guy appeared a little nervous when he reached into his pocket to make change. Even the lady in the parking spot beside him at the drugstore seemed to hold her stare at him just a bit too long. Everyone and everything seemed to invite suspicion and suggest danger, not just for Rick, but for his wife and kids too.

> To live like Jesus is to have people respond to us as they would Jesus.

When federal agencies confirmed the written threats were real and to be taken seriously, the stakes were raised. Rick could hardly process thoughts of his family being harmed because of his efforts to expand the work of Christ among the churches. It didn't seem right on so many levels. Within a few months, Rick was admitted to the hospital and began receiving treatment for symptoms brought on by a stress-related illness. And while he never would have chosen to be so significantly sidetracked by stress, the days of physician-prescribed rest gave him plenty of time to think and consider the ramifications and consequences if he *did* or *didn't* remain true to his principles and his vision of kingdom building that included everyone—regardless of their color.

In the end, Rick recovered from his illness and received a clean bill of health. With renewed health and a reinvigorated commitment, Rick returned to his position and continued spreading the Word of God on being all-inclusive, handling the haters as they came, and dealing with the dissenters in the ranks.

It's not always easy, but it's what Jesus would do, and it is precisely the kind of persecution He warned could (and probably would) come the way of the peacemaker. By the way, this series of events happened in the late 1990s, not the late 1890s.

The final characteristic of a new way of living, *persecution* is the sum of all the other Beatitudes. To *live* like Jesus is to have people *respond* to us as they would Jesus—sometimes welcoming and gracious, sometimes violently opposed, and many times, tepidly, without conviction one way or the other.

The People

Jesus congratulated those who experienced persecution for living like Him. Of all His blessings, this one may seem the strangest, if not completely paradoxical. Ours isn't the first generation to ask, "*How is it a blessing to suffer for doing what God wants?*" Who would expect to be insulted, mocked, or ostracized for doing the very things God directs us to do? Shouldn't it work the other way around? Doesn't it make you want to ask, "*What's wrong with this picture?*"

Although it does seem odd that doing the very thing Jesus

calls us to do leads to resistance rather than acceptance, it is one of the certainties of establishing the kingdom of God "on earth as it is in heaven": as you follow Jesus, you will be treated like Jesus. Peacemaking is both trying and tiring, but Jesus promises to bless peacemakers in their righteous fatigue.

Hurtful accusations, affronts to integrity, and questions of motives are all part of the work of being salt and light servants—and those are some of the lesser examples of war wounds the faithful endure! Bruises of all kinds—physical, verbal, and emotional—are sometimes the mark of following Jesus. The negative responses of friends and family are frequently sound validation that we are making progress in the casualty-rich arena of peacemaking.

In the end, it is helpful to remember that Jesus came to establish a new covenant with God's people. Amazingly, His gift of redemption, the forgiveness of sins, and the promise of eternity with Him was met with more than a little resistance by many of the key influencers of the time. The reason? These honor-lovin', my-robe-is-longer-than-yours kind of religious leaders knew that to accept and follow Jesus contradicted everything they stood for, legislated, and enforced. Since Jesus as the Messiah, the fulfillment of the Torah and the new Temple, were the underlying realities of Christ's ministry and since these truths had little place in the expectations of the Pharisees and Sadducees, to accept one was to reject the other. If Jesus was right, they weren't just wrong; they were out of a job, void of their title, and ditched of their prestigious positions. The compassionate *and* indicting words of Jesus as the Promised One had no place in the lives of those comfortable with the way things were. The result: Jesus faced persecution every step of the way as He brought the peace and presence of God to those who would receive it.

The Characteristic

Jesus knew the truth of His blessing. He knew who sent Him, why He came, and even His eventual, tortuous conclusion on earth. He also knew the glorious reunion that awaited all who endured persecution on His behalf. This undoubtedly explains why, time after time, Jesus responded confidently and quietly to the sneers and jeers of those blatantly opposed to His teachings.

Consider a few of the instances where Jesus endured taunts, threats, and indignities at the hands of those who doubted or felt threatened by His words:

- Upon coming to revive the ruler's dead young daughter, the onlookers laughed at Him yet Jesus did not attack (Matthew 9:23–26).

- When Jesus healed the man's shriveled hand *in* the synagogue *on* the Sabbath as fulfillment of the prophet Isaiah's words, the Pharisees began plotting to kill Him, yet He stood His ground and challenged their legalistic perspective (Matthew 12:13–14).
- As he returned to His hometown of Nazareth and was doubted, discounted, and almost run off a cliff, He peacefully and calmly left on His own terms (Luke 4:22–30).
- And finally, when the high priest demanded He reply to the charges of His accusers, Jesus said simply, "Yes, it is as you say" (Matthew 26:64) and quietly allowed His Father's will to be fulfilled (Matthew 26:62–65).

Peace in the midst of persecution is a sign that God reigns in a person's heart. It is also the evidence of the Holy Spirit reigning in the heart of a person (Galatians 5:22). Enduring slander, insults, and attacks from others is as much a hallmark of a follower of Jesus as showing mercy or being meek. This apparent contradiction goes against our reasoning because we are quick to *naturally* assume that becoming more like Jesus will lead to less, not more, conflicts and confrontations. But remember, Jesus said peacemaking on His behalf sometimes involves a sword that cuts through existing relationships as we seek to live out newfound or newly recharged commitments (Matthew 10:34–37).

RESISTANCE TO YOUR PHYSICAL HEALTH GOALS

Throughout our study of Jesus' sermon, we have sought to align the disciplines of the Beatitudes with the discipline of pursuing physical wellness. While one addresses our spiritual well-being and the other our physical, there exist several similarities between the two. One of the qualities integral to both kinds of wellness is *resistance training.*

Just as this final verse in the Beatitudes promises a heavenly reward for endurance, inherent in this promise is also the understanding that believers will have to encounter, withstand, and triumph through persecution. We can't be permanently discouraged when we meet up with someone who criticizes our Christ-centered beliefs. We can't abandon the call to share the Gospel when we are not met with receptive responses. And we can't cave in to questions and personal attacks when we know we're doing the right thing in Christ's eyes. We have to lean more into our relationship with our Leader in order to counter the resistance with commitment. The more we stand with Him to love those who persecute us, the stronger we become in every way.

The same is true for pursuing physical strength. We can't stop at one circuit of weights because it hurts. We can't hope for defined and sculpted muscle tone without pressing past what is easy for us. And we can't hope to build endurance and strength if we don't regularly and systematically show up, do the repetitions (reps), and push through the temporary discomfort. The more we consistently exercise our muscles, the more prepared they will be to serve us in time of need, illness, or competition.

See the similarities? Resistance, while not enjoyable at the time, usually results in greater strength, improved flexibility, and increased endurance—all-important factors whether you're debating with a nonbeliever or climbing to the top of a 14er in Colorado.

On the physical front, resistance training is an integral part of training necessary to run long distances. It can be done in several ways. One method uses weights to provide resistance to the muscles. Through reps you repeatedly push against weights and then return to the starting position. This overextension of your muscle actually tears the fibrous tissue of your muscles microscopically. When you rest a day or two between resistance exercises, the torn fibers heal and are stronger than they were before the workout. Repeat this process and you build strength upon strength.

> There is a relevant and practical daily application.

AN ACCEPTED CONSEQUENCE

As a precursor to what would become a life of sacrifice and persecution, the man who later was known as the Apostle Paul was a witness at the execution of Stephen, the first martyr of the early church movement. After raining pain upon the small groups of Christ followers and becoming a follower of the risen Lord, Paul considered persecution an acceptable consequence for the honor of living out God's call on his life. It was simply a given, not *if* it happens, but *when* it does—like having a crash on your bike if you ride far and hard enough. Paul even seemed to eagerly anticipate the opportunity to be persecuted on Christ's behalf. It was an honor and one he took quiet seriously. Paul saw succeeding through resistance as the way followers of Jesus revealed the life of Christ in themselves. For Paul, if you weren't up for a little imprisonment or a few floggings, what good was your testimony of Christ's impact on your life? (Read 2 Corinthians 6:3–10 for Paul's list of some of his hardships.)

In our ramped-up, teched-up, feel-no-pain modern culture, pain and suffering for *anything* is usually too costly. Isn't there a drug for that? Can't we just avoid the pain? Why must it all be so confrontational?

In the kingdom, however, suffering for righteousness allows us to give evidence that we are citizens of His kingdom. Suffering says that we've been bought, paid for, and are indebted eternally—whatever the cost. That's why, while we may not be stoned to death for our beliefs like Stephen or we may never have to defend them in a court of law like Paul (in some countries, followers of Jesus *do* face these realities), we should accept, prepare for and, dare I say, embrace resistance if we are to wholeheartedly follow Christ. Anything less is unacceptable.

The Promise

Jesus made a never-to-be-matched-again promise to those who were persecuted for following Him. He declared "the kingdom of heaven is theirs." With this promise we come full circle in Jesus' blessings to His followers. Remember this is the same promise He made in the first beatitude to those poor in spirit, those who had realized their spiritual poverty.

I see in this round-trip from valley to summit to valley another facet of the Beatitudes: spiritual health follows a path to maturity. In fact, upon closer inspection, it's not a far stretch to view the challenges and promises as a worthwhile plan for my daily life. See if my daily routine doesn't resemble much of yours: before my feet hit the floor in the morning I need to recognize my dependence on Christ, which establishes my poverty of spirit. I then need to repent (or become mournful) of my sins and surrender control of my life to Him as an act of honorable meekness. And so on. All the way through each of the Beatitudes, there is a relevant and practical daily application that ultimately culminates in our willingness to be faithful even in the face of hostility.

But Jesus went beyond the simple promise of heaven as a reward to the faithful and the persecuted. In the two verses following His promise, He expanded upon His blessing: "Blessed are you when people insult you, persecute you and falsely say all kinds of evil against you because of me. Rejoice and be glad, because great is your reward in heaven, for in the same way they persecuted the prophets who were before you" (Matthew 5:11–12). His words were a warning *and* a promise to His disciples then just as they are a warning and a promise to His followers today. He wanted them (and us) to know the

reward for enduring persecution was great: membership in the kingdom of God.

Jesus promised that persecution and resistance showed that you are on His team. Confront the office bully about how he treats the janitorial crew and bear the wrath of his considerable anger and risk becoming the next target of his ridicule. Congratulations! You've just lettered in persecution.

Call into question the way your sister berates her children and bring on a three-week silent treatment. Way to go! You've earned a bar for your letter jacket.

Stand before the city council and plead for city funds to be invested in a poor neighborhood which has been overlooked year after year only to find you are the only advocate for those families. Consider yourself blessed. You just made the starting lineup of the persecuted all-stars!

How we respond when we are persecuted for our faith in Christ is truly where the rubber meets the road in terms of our actions backing up our words. Sure, it's easy to speak of Christ's love in the presence of your Bible study group. It's even easy to speak of how you were blessed by someone's kindness to nonbelievers. But let somebody get all up in your face—literally or figuratively—about being a religious troublemaker and then it's time to put your money where your mouth is. Jesus blesses us when we are persecuted because we are willing to take a stand on His behalf and do whatever it takes to stay strong in the face of attack for His kingdom purposes.

Resistance training is to running what persecution is to spiritual health.

PERSECUTION BUILDS SPIRITUAL MUSCLE

Resistance training is to running what persecution is to spiritual health; it is pushing past what is easy and comfortable in order to strengthen a muscle. In a similar manner, persecution builds strength in our spiritual muscles. In the Book of James, the author has the remarkable ability to make persecution almost desirable, or, if not desirable, at least honorable. Read his words and see if you don't agree that this guy writes some pretty persuasive copy: "Consider it pure joy, my brothers, whenever you face trials of many kinds, because you know that the testing of your faith develops perseverance. . . . Blessed is the man who perseveres under trial, because when he has stood the test, he will receive the crown of life that God has promised to those who love him" (James 1:2–3, 12). The word for *perseverance* in this first verse is the same one that can be translated "endurance" in Hebrews 12:1, "Let us run with *endurance* the race marked out for us" (NASB). The word literally means to "bear up under the weight."

Endurance in running, for example, is the ability to bear up under the weight of fatigue brought on by distance, terrain, and weather conditions. Endurance as a peacemaker is the ability to bear up under the weight of persecution, lack of immediate results, and spiritual fatigue caused by a lifelong commitment to finish the race Jesus has marked out for you. Endurance isn't easy; it's not particularly enjoyable at the time; and it's not for the shortsighted. Endurance is for finish-line thinkers and those with an eternity-tinted lens.

Jesus promised that those who gained strength from withstanding the harassment of their enemies belonged in His kingdom. The higher the level of disgust, resentment, and wrath you can withstand, the further you are along the path to spiritual health and maturity. Not that you should or would look for areas to stir up controversy—that's not the point. Become recognized as a child of God through your peacemaking actions, and you won't have to look for a fight; the fight will ensue when you expose darkness or upset the status quo. Your job is not to shy away from confrontation when it's presented. For the mature believer, this means you are ready, willing, and able to defend your faith and your Father when circumstances present themselves—regardless of the cost.

The Illness

Facing persecution is difficult, sometimes painful, and can even be life-threatening. Though we don't often experience it here in our country, thousands, if not millions, of people across the globe suffer all kinds of persecution at all kinds of levels. Religious persecution is the most pervasive, but ethnic persecution, based on a people's heritage, is frequently imposed also.

Twenty-first-century Americans can't truly grasp the gravity of what it means to suffer for the cause of Christ, especially to the point of death. But for first-century believers, persecution was a given. For them, it was not out of the norm to be beaten, stoned, mocked, slandered, threatened, and/or imprisoned for refusing to denounce their faith. Because they confessed "Jesus is Lord" rather than "Caesar is Lord," they knew persecution was sure to follow. It was a condition of the faith, but one they honorably accepted for the privilege of following Him.

The most common misguided reactions to modern-day persecution include giving up by foregoing the fight and forgetting the faith, developing a martyr complex, or pushing ourselves beyond reasonable personal limitations. Let's look at each of these a bit deeper.

GIVING UP

Being a believer doesn't necessarily mean you have to develop a fight-or-flight mindset. Just because you can't cite verse after verse of Scripture supporting your every belief doesn't mean you shouldn't stand up for what you know, what you've witnessed, and what you've personally experienced. No contrary arguments can discount these.

The writer of the Letter to the Hebrews knew the importance of not giving up in the "struggle against sin." The writer acknowledged his readers had "not yet resisted to the point of shedding [their] blood," in their struggle but they were to "endure hardship as discipline" from God who loved them like a father (Hebrews 12:4, 7). He told them that this discipline would produce "a harvest of righteousness and peace," for those who had been "trained by it" (v. 11). We get our English word *gymnasium* from the root word in the Greek for the verb *to train*. God's discipline is like going to a spiritual gym to strengthen our faith. He then encouraged them to "strengthen your feeble arms and weak knees. 'Make level paths for your feet,' so that the lame may not be disabled, but rather healed" (Hebrews 12:12–14). We will not give up when faced with resistance from others when we are made strong through our relationship with God in Christ Jesus.

If the first time someone threatens you with trouble if you don't drop the subject causes you never to return to that person's need for Christ, that would be tragic. I remember a woman who looked me in the eye and told me in no uncertain terms, "When I want your help, I'll ask for it. Until then, keep out of my life." It wasn't necessarily a friendly exchange, but I had committed, along with her husband, to be part of a team that worked to restore her to the mother and wife she had previously been and that God wanted her to be. She was spiraling downward at a frightening rate and her husband and I thought it wise not to wait for an invitation from her for help. At times it got a bit contentious, but we stayed the course and, eventually, God changed her heart.

MARTYR COMPLEX

A second unacceptable response to full-out persecution resembles developing a martyr complex. A true martyr is

> Maturing in a relationship is not the same as strengthening in endurance.

someone who gives up his life as a witness to Jesus' death on the Cross like Stephen, who was the first to be martyred for his witness to Jesus. We get our English word *martyr* from the Greek word usually translated "witness." (See Acts 22:15.) Eventually, most of the apostles (including Paul) were martyred for their allegiance to Christ. The difference between *being* an actual martyr and *assuming* a martyr complex is dramatic. One (the martyr) actually suffers, sometimes to the point of death, while the other (those with the martyr complex) develops an attitude that uses real or perceived persecution to draw attention to themselves. People with martyr complexes tend to remind everyone how hard their life in Christ, or in general, really is. They often dominate a prayer time with troubles others have shown them. Resistance from others is part of following Jesus; it results in spiritual strength, not the self-absorption of self-centered attention.

PUSHING TOO HARD

A third manner of mishandling persecution results in pushing ourselves beyond our capacities. Just as runners get into trouble when they press beyond their training and capabilities, so do Christians. This is especially the case when they continue to engage in peacemaking when they are not trained sufficiently or do not have the spiritual capacity for difficult conflicts. When Jesus sent out His disciples, He told them, "If anyone will not welcome you or listen to your words, shake the dust off your feet when you leave that home or town" (Matthew 10:14). Jesus taught His followers to be prudent as they spread the work of His kingdom. He also taught them not to resist those who attacked them. In fact, He told them to love their enemies and "pray for those who persecute" them (Matthew 5:44). God's people should neither meet resistance with resistance nor push others to follow Him.

The Exercise

No single spiritual exercise can produce in you the strength to bear up under the weight of persecution. To be prepared is to develop a variety of spiritual disciplines that address the many different aspects of persecution. You know that lifting weights alone cannot prepare you for a marathon; likewise choosing

prayer as your only spiritual exercise does not adequately prepare you to endure every type of resistance involved in peacemaking.

When God has transformed your heart and life to the place where you can engage others with the peace of God, you must be able to bear up under the weight of resistance—both emotionally and spiritually. This comes only as you participate in a balanced, effective program of spiritual training. I apply the same principle when developing a training program for peak performance for race day. My training program involves frequency, duration, and intensity of preparation based upon the time I have allotted to train for the race. My success in the race is directly related to my discipline to complete the training program.

In the same way you can adopt a program for spiritual growth. A word of caution: *maturing in a relationship is not the same as strengthening in endurance.* Keep in mind that my suggested spiritual exercise program is only an analogy of how to make the disciplines an integral part of your deepening spirituality. It is not a guarantee and certainly involves more than just systematically checking off assigned readings or contrived efforts at ministry.

That said, as I mentioned, I do believe in the wisdom of at least plotting out some semblance of *a spiritual training program to be used as a guide*, but one that remains flexible enough to be led by the Holy Spirit.

As a starting point, let me suggest you identify four of the spiritual exercises that stood out to you in this book. Now, take a month-long calendar (the kind with boxes large enough to write inside) and assign each of the four different spiritual exercises to one of the four available Sundays. Next assign a related goal on each of the days following each individual exercise. For example, if you selected *silence and solitude* for the first Sunday of the month, then you might write something like *20 minutes/twice a day* in each of the following weekday boxes. This would mean that for one week you would practice silence and solitude two times a day without any other agenda or goals. For 20 minutes a day, twice a day, you would shut off the outside noise that clutters so much of our lives and allow the silence to speak to you and refresh your soul. Interesting concept, isn't it?

To ensure your commitment remains a priority and not just something hoped for, *enlist an accountability partner* to keep you on track. I would sleep in many mornings and not work out if I did not know there was someone waiting to join me at the agreed upon time and place. Jesus knew what He was doing when He sent His disciples out two by two (Mark 6:7).

After each time you practice the assigned discipline, *write a brief note on the date explaining what God taught you during this time.* Like an exercise log that records your physical progress toward your goal, these notes or journal will record your deepening relationship with God and the impact it has on others and on you. Sometimes God will speak volumes, enlighten your mind, and flood your soul with insight and avenues for growth; other times He will allow the exercise itself to be sufficient instruction for the day. Either way, the cumulative effect of maintaining a regular commitment to strengthening your relationship with God will not go without reward.

Your growth and development may seem almost imperceptible at the time, but trust that each effort you make toward growing your relationship with God will result in a greater and more effective influence your witness will have on those He places in your path. Keep in mind that the ultimate motivation is not for you to change yourself, but for God to prepare you for service in His kingdom. In doing so, the final glory will be His.

Takeaway

The final step on our spiritual journey is to face persecution for the work of peacemaking we do in the name of Jesus. To live and love like Jesus is to accept the response of people like those who responded to Jesus: with open hearts and with plots to kill. Jesus promised that those who were persecuted for the sake of His name would gain the kingdom of heaven. What a reward for the work of living as one of Jesus' disciples! In order to hold up during times of resistance, you must be strong spiritually. A spiritual training program that incorporates multiple disciplines and practices is necessary to endure the onslaught of resistance by those who oppose Jesus and His kingdom way of life.

Questions for Reflection

1. Do you know of someone like Rick who has suffered persecution for his or her peacemaking among a group of people or community? Write out the name(s) and circumstances. What qualities of Jesus did you see in them as they went through this trial?

2. How have you faced persecution or resistance because of your peacemaking practices? Write out your circumstances here. How were you able to endure the experience?

3. What exercise plans have you tried and how successful were you with them?

4. Will you create the "spiritual exercise program" suggested in this book? What spiritual disciplines will you begin to develop in your life? Write them here and recruit an accountability partner to help you succeed with your intentions.

CHAPTER 11

(FINAL) TAKEAWAY

Be perfect, therefore, as your heavenly Father is perfect.

—MATTHEW 5:48

After blessing His disciples with the Beatitudes, Jesus told them they were to "be perfect . . . as your heavenly Father is perfect" (Matthew 5:48). He had already said enough that day to give them plenty of things to talk about around the dinner table that night—things like love your enemies, be happy when people insult you, and if lust is an issue for you, poke out those traitorous eyeballs! But perfection? Isn't that setting the bar just a bit too high?

Well, yes.

And, no.

Think about it. You don't ever set a goal at being just so-so at something, do you? It's not like they give out blue ribbons or trophies for being mediocre at things. And the last time I checked, halfhearted efforts were rarely, if ever, considered honorable and praiseworthy. Think how that might sound if you were introducing one friend to another: "Sam, this is Charlie. Charlie is a so-so husband, an occasional friend, and a minimally involved father." Kind of makes you want to run the other way, doesn't it?

Or imagine some moms at the fourth-grade Christmas program talking about their kid's performance:

> The intent was not moral perfection or flawlessness.

"So, Jenny, which one is yours?"

"Mine? Oh, mine is the third snowflake from the left. Yes, we're occasionally proud of him, but for the most part, he's very mediocre!"

Huh? What about the salesman pitching his best product? Do you think he'd hype his product and then pronounce it just so-so? Not if he was working on commission!

See what I mean when I say aiming for anything less than perfection is a short-sighted, self-fulfilling prophecy? Shoot for the bottom rung on the ladder, and that's most likely where you'll land.

But with Christ, it's different.

For me, for you, in all that we do, perfection should be the highest goal in any arena of our lives—physically, spiritually, mentally, and emotionally. Daunting and overwhelming? You betcha! Even unattainable? Definitely. But goal-worthy? Without a doubt!

Consider striving for perfection in your physical wellness and let the excuses begin:

"Be perfect? Are you serious?"

"I can't make my workouts every day!"

"I can't stop eating chocolate-covered almonds!"

"Be perfect? What kind of fitness nut are you? Only the people who love to watch themselves lift weights in the mirror at the gym shoot for perfection. I'm a weekend warrior, not a professional athlete."

And since the quest for spiritual perfection seems just as absurd to most of us, it hardly seems worth the effort when you consider the endless opportunities to sin before sunset each day. It's enough to make you ask, "What kind of spiritual leader is Jesus really if He demands perfection from me?"

I believe those who heard Jesus explain what life was like in His kingdom were probably as taken aback *then* at His demand for perfection as we are *today* when faced with the same challenge. *Perfection*? Really? What some of the people 2,000-plus years ago and some of us today fail to understand is that He was not demanding the same thing as what *we* consider perfection.

While all the major translations of the Bible stick with the English word *perfect* for Jesus' call to follow Him and His ways, *the intent was not moral perfection or flawlessness.* Jesus wanted His followers to respond in love to their enemies as perfectly and as fully as God responds in love to them (Matthew 5:43–48). Yes, Jesus called His followers to be perfect, but that completeness was to show itself in love just as our "heavenly Father is perfect" in love. When we understand this, at least perfection is not some vague, illusive concept, but rather a more specific, more clearly defined concept. Now, the challenge is to understand and embrace how we do that.

Part of being *perfect* like the Father is simply *being like* Him. The Beatitudes reveal not only whom we are to become, but also *what God-in-Jesus looks like*. Jesus blessed those who were like Him and longed to

> Our goal in following Jesus is to live and love like Him.

live as God called them to live. Look again at the list of characteristics in Jesus' words:

Poor in Spirit (humble)
Mournful (healthy mourning)
Meek
To hunger and thirst for righteousness
Merciful
Pure in heart
As a peacemaker
Persecuted for bringing God's peace

Don't these describe Jesus and the heart of God that He lived out in His life on earth? Didn't Jesus reveal Himself in those

He blessed and in what He promised they would receive? Yes. And yes. So, to be perfect, complete or full in living like Jesus, it follows that we are best able to display these characteristics if the basis for our lives is a trusting relationship with Him—an ongoing, ever-evolving, ever-deepening relationship. Think about how it is for a golfer to better his game: repeated strokes lead to enhanced muscle memory which leads to improved, second nature performance. This is exactly what happens when we remain focused on and engaged in a moment-by-moment trusting relationship with Him.

Allow me to answer some questions you may have about how we can live such a life and experience what Jesus has taught us.

Why **shoot for perfection?**

I am amazed at the quality of professional athletes and the tiny differences that separate their performances. Olympic swimmers win by .001 of a second. Golfers lose a million dollars because of a missed four-foot putt. Whether baseball players hit a foul ball or home run is determined by a millisecond when a 95 mph fastball crosses the plate. Near perfection (and sometimes even complete perfection) in sports competition is a given in order to be considered a world-class athlete. But if you and I are not one of these perfectly sculpted, perfectly pitching, or perfectly poised stellar athletes, why should we even be talking about perfection?

> Spiritual wellness comes from a lifestyle built on the choices we make.

First, remember *perfect* in Jesus' call to His disciples *does not mean moral perfection or flawlessness*! Our goal in following Jesus is to live and love like Him, not be religiously perfect. The way we do this is by living in a daily trusting and deepening relationship with Him. Our goal should always be to demonstrate in all our interactions with others the same suffering and sacrificial love that God first showed us in Christ Jesus. Be mindful of this distinction and remember that we do not shoot for perfection in keeping religious rules, but in showing people God's love in tangible ways like loving fully our enemies instead of just loving those who love us. This one solitary act will set us apart as true followers of Jesus like nothing else.

The *why* for our spiritual wellness is our desire to share the love He has shown us with others. John simply states, "We love because he first loved us" (1 John 4:19). We are loved by God, forgiven by the sacrifice of the Son, empowered by the Holy Spirit, and so *we love, forgive, and empower others in His name.* Just as the golfer hits 100 sand shots in an afternoon in order to get "up and down" out of a trap in the next tournament, we also practice the spiritual disciplines in order to love, forgive, and empower others as peacemakers in the name of Jesus. We train to be like Jesus through spiritual exercises so that the Holy Spirit's strength and power will flow through us as we love and serve others in the name of Jesus.

Wellness is not an add-on to your lifestyle. It is your lifestyle.

When do we work out toward these goals?

When do we work for the spiritual realities Jesus taught in the Beatitudes? The answer is: morning, noon, and night. "What? You want me to quit my job and go to a monastery?" There was a time in church history when that was the answer, but I have a better idea. Just as physical wellness is the result of a *lifestyle* of health, in the same way spiritual wellness comes from a *lifestyle* built on the choices we make hour by hour. Physical health is the result of a 24/7 lifestyle of diet, rest, and activity. People fail to reach their goals of spiritual health because they *separate their health-focused eating, rest, and activities from their daily lifestyles.* We go to the gym before work and then take the elevator to the fourth floor office. We eat a health bar and apple for lunch so we can then pig out and have dessert for dinner. *Wellness is not an add-on to your lifestyle. It is your lifestyle.*

For example, a healthy diet—and you already know this—includes lean meats (if you eat meat), vegetables, fruit, and whole grains. Cut out the processed sugars and flours—the white stuff—and you are on the way to allowing your body to perform as it was created to perform. However, one healthy meal a day does not make a healthy body if you eat a candy bar after the other two. Whether you adjust to six small meals a day or cut back on portions in the three our culture says you should eat, eating healthy is not a once-every-three-months-to-lose-five-pounds routine. It does not come as a result of an hour-and-a-half "muscle confusion" workout that you do for 90 days and then quit. If that was the answer, what happens on days 91, 100, 300? This is why diets work for a while but most people regain the pounds they lost because they never changed *how* and *why* they ate what got them overweight in the first place. People complete the plan but few adopt a *lifestyle* of wellness that is necessary for permanent change.

Spiritual wellness comes in the same way. If you practice your spiritual exercises—like prayer, for example—first thing in the morning but don't converse with God throughout the day, then you find limited strength or guidance from His presence. If you only go to the spiritual gym you call church for either a worship service or a small group gathering once or twice a week and don't interact with fellow followers of Jesus any other time, then you will lose your focus on spiritual wellness and your ability to live it out to honor God throughout the week. If you only "eat this book" (Ezekiel 3:1–3) of God's Word on weekends or when you are in a bind, you will never know what it is to grow in strength from knowing the Author of the book. If you only give what's in your wallet when the offering basket comes by, you will never know the joy of sacrificial giving to help change the life of another.

Spiritual wellness, like physical wellness, must be worked out in the ebb and flow of daily life. If you only do it when you feel like it, those times can be few and far between. Be mindful, spiritual warrior, that the spiritual exercises mentioned in this book are for *daily* use. Consider the following and see if you can't come up with a few of your own:

- Skip a meal and read the Bible instead during mealtime.
- Pray for a friend while you're on a break.
- Find solitude in your office and listen for the Holy Spirit to speak to you about what you are doing that day.
- Leave the building for a meal or break, sit in a park and pray for those who walk by you.
- Get out of the car in the carpool line at school and meet the parents in cars behind you.
- Integrate spiritual practices into your daily decisions and activities and you will begin to see differences in your attitudes and actions toward others almost immediately.

The *when* of spiritual wellness is *every day* in *every way* you live.

Where do we practice the spiritual exercises and the Beatitudes they develop?

In a culture that provides just about any imaginable goods and service to those who can afford them, many people believe they have to be a member of a gym or health club to become "fit." However, if we only exercise in a gym or health club outside the home or daily work, we are less likely to develop a lifestyle of physical strength and health. I am a member of a fitness club, but I found that going there takes time and effort that I could be using to be fit!

A while back, I was sharing climbing stories with a group of guys over dinner, and one of them began to tell how he walked and cycled to his office. (This was in the middle of his tales of summiting 24,000-foot mountains in Peru and Ecuador.) Out of the blue, he said, "I just like to walk." For some reason that phrase struck at my heart. I like to walk, too, but my lifestyle was to drive to a park or hill and walk there. I would plan for months for a weeklong climb or hike while never walking in my neighborhood. Or, I would drive to a parking lot, get my bike out of the car, ride, put the bike back in my car and drive home. It hit me as I drove home from that dinner, "Why don't *you* walk or ride your bike to *your* office?" I reasoned that when I travel in walking-oriented countries such as China or Vietnam, for example, I walk. So, why don't I walk at home?

As a result of that conversation, when I know I will be in the office all day or if I can ask people to come pick me up for a lunch appointment or walk to the corner coffee shop, I walk or ride my bike to work. The three-and-one-half-mile walk (or ride) one way has become a time of prayer, praise, and planning for the day. Why didn't I think of that earlier? I had separated the *where* of my exercise to a fitness club, and I had not integrated it into everyday living. I believed the car, not my feet, was the primary mode of transportation where I live.

The *where* of spiritual exercises is similar to the *when*. Just as the *when* of spiritual health is a 24/7 lifestyle, the *where* of spiritual wellness and vitality is anywhere God has planted or led you. If we limit our spiritual exercises to sacred places or to our homes, we miss sharing the love of God like Jesus did—which was wherever He went with whomever He met.

At Legacy Church we state our mission as: "We help people trust Jesus as the church, at home, and in the world." Those last three phrases are what I call our "arenas of faith." Those are the *where* we help people trust Jesus. *As the church* we gather

> An injury or illness forces you to stop, assess, and rebuild.

to worship, reach, connect, grow, and serve as the rescued ones. Notice we did not write *at* the church. The church is a people, not a place. We see our lives connected in a network of relationships unique to our lives. God uses those relational connections as potential bridges of influence to show others the love of God in tangible ways. As the gathered and scattered people of God, the church, we live as witnesses in word and actions to those God has put in our network of family, friends, co-workers, and acquaintances.

At home is another arena in which we intentionally help people trust Jesus. We seek to establish the values of love, submission, honor, and training in our relationships at home. As the church we partner with parents to nurture their children toward trusting Jesus. We believe the home is the primary disciple-making unit of the church and God intends for every parent to be a spiritual leader to his or her child in order to nurture them into followers of Jesus who live and love like Him. The *where* of disciple making includes your home.

In the world is anywhere God has planted or sent us. The world begins next door to where you live and extends around the globe. Where we live, learn, work and play are our mission fields to serve and love others in the name of Jesus. We are a sent people to those who are lost in order to be a blessing to all people.

The *where* of spiritual wellness is everywhere God leads or places us and in every relationship in our network of friends, families, and co-workers. Jesus engaged people wherever He went, and He intentionally shared the love of the Father with whomever He encountered. Just as physical wellness flows out of the *where* of everyday life, in the same way the *where* of spiritual wellness is wherever God leads us that day.

What does this journey look like for me in real life?

The journey to spiritual wellness or maturity is more akin to a hike on the Bluff Mountain Trail off the Blue Ridge Parkway than a drive on Interstate 85 from Atlanta to Charlotte. In other words, the path will be long and winding; it will become frighteningly narrow at points; and there'll be several washouts and roadblocks along the way. You may even be tempted to turn around and run the other way more than once. Jesus knew this firsthand and that is why just beyond the message of the Beatitudes He taught His disciples that "small is the gate and narrow the road that leads to life, and only a few find it" (Matthew 7:13–14). Just as relatively few see the world from the top of a 6,000-foot peak in North Carolina, few in numbers go through the narrow gate and take the even narrower road to spiritual maturity. Sadly, our society has come to value speed over meaning and ease over struggle in order to obtain whatever it is we're after—including personal growth. It should come as no surprise that this same realignment of values has seeped into how we see spiritual growth and how we go about achieving it.

I'm the first to accept that not everyone reading this book can hike mountain paths to a magnificent summit. But, let's remember that before the invention of motorized vehicles, we walked or rode animals to get where we were going just like Jesus walked and rode animals. My point is not to bash motorized machines—I wouldn't want to live without them—but I want to remind us that most of the world does not own a car, and they *still* walk or ride animals every day.

My point *is* to say that walking slows us down to see the trees, hear the birds, and talk to people as we pass. Those things cannot happen when we spend significant parts of our days enclosed in our cubicles-on-wheels, speeding to get wherever we need to be on time. While hiking you see vistas and valleys you can't see from the interstate that brought you there. When walking in your city, you can see and pray for needs and people you would not be aware of as you drive by listening to the radio with the windows rolled up.

Your journey to live and love like Jesus will, most likely, be slower than the pace you're living now. It will also be more off the main roads you travel to get to and from your overscheduled appointments. There are simply no nonstop tollways to Christian maturity. While we can't sell everything and start walking everywhere we go, we can consider a spiritual journey that is slower and on different paths than we are on now. Our hunger and thirst for the presence of God will cause us to stop long enough to be filled with His presence and righteousness in order to complete the journey He has called us to complete.

Let me say a word about injuries or setbacks. As I am writing this chapter I am wearing a therapeutic boot on my right foot. I have been running, riding, walking and hiking on a stress fracture since last June (OK, it's May.) Knowing that pain is the body's way of saying "Help!" I continued to "run through the pain" until my body said, "Not one more step until you take care of me." Injuries happen. You may choose to be foolish (or as I prefer to see it, *persistent*!) and cause an injury to worsen. At the very least, you will undoubtedly encounter accidents, injuries, and strains as you stretch yourself to your limit. So, is there any value in these injuries, illness, or setbacks? Absolutely yes!

Since I must wear the boot and stay off my foot for a minimum of four weeks, I have more time to write, which is my first love and a significant part of God's call on my life to equip people to know, share, and multiply Christ. Injured, I have more time to rest, which will aid in my recovery *and* long-term health. Cutting back on my activities means I must focus more on my diet, and I am forced back into the swimming pool, one of the best overall exercises for the body but the weakest of all my sport activities.

Several years ago, an IT-band injury caused by overuse forced me to stop running and to start swimming. That injury led me to discover the sport of sprint triathlons, a multidiscipline sport that is much more fun than some of the long-distance, concrete-pounding runs I was doing before my injury. Injuries or illness can slow you down and open new venues you would not find if you had otherwise stayed healthy and maintained the same routine. In fact, just by staying on the same workout path and never introducing a bit of variety, you'll inevitably work yourself into a rut and diminish the effectiveness of your workout.

An injury or illness forces you to stop, assess, and rebuild. While I would prefer not to be ill or have an injury, such times force me to *stop* my current routine that caused the injury, *assess* how or why the injury happened, and *rebuild* my lifestyle with a new perspective on health and

The Bible calls this expectancy hope.

activity. These bumps in the road can be blessings in disguise for one seeking physical wellness.

Spiritual injuries, illnesses, and accidents can produce similar results. An injury caused by word or action, while you go about the business of making peace in the valley of relationships, may cause you to *stop* what you were saying or doing, *assess* the cause of the injurious act or word, and *rebuild* the relationship in a fresh and Holy Spirit–renewed way so God will be honored through it. Spiritual warfare, persecution, and fatigue can bring you to a halt and force you to find new ways of being a peacemaker where you live, learn, work, or play.

Suffering or spiritual injury always has a greater purpose. Paul encouraged his friends in Corinth to consider their "troubles" and God's "comfort" toward them as ways to comfort

others who experience the same things. He wrote,

> *Praise be to the God and Father of our Lord Jesus Christ, the Father of compassion and the God of all comfort, who comforts us in all our troubles, so that we can comfort those in any trouble with the comfort we ourselves receive from God. For just as the sufferings of Christ flow over into our lives, so also through Christ our comfort overflows. If we are distressed, it is for your comfort and salvation; if we are comforted, it is for your comfort, which produces in you patient endurance of the same sufferings we suffer. And our hope for you is firm, because we know that just as you share in our sufferings, so also you share in our comfort.*
>
> —2 Corinthians 1:3–7

As we experience the healing love of Christ in our lives, we can help others who are injured and come to us for advice because we have had the same hurt. We can encourage those who suffer spiritually because we have known the same pain and received God's comfort and strength.

Your journey to spiritual wellness will show you new vistas and valleys of God's leading and surprise you with the power and hope the Holy Spirit will give you along the way.

What can I expect by practicing the Beatitudes every day?

When you climb, you expect to reach the summit. When you step up to the starting line of a 5K run, you expect to see the finish line. If weight loss is your goal, you expect to see a certain number on a scale someday. And, if a renewed relationship with a loved one is your goal, you hope to see a smiling face across the table sometime. Every worthy endeavor has a goal or finish line, and in order to realize those things you live *a life of expectancy*. The Bible calls this expectancy *hope*. The Holy Spirit inspired Paul to explain that hope is a result of suffering, struggles that we face as we live out our made-right lives with God (Romans 5:1–5). Because we know the summit of our climb is "peace with God," we live with *a hope-filled certainty* that we will experience that summit, both on earth and in heaven. We can face suffering or struggles related to being peacemakers as Jesus called us to be *because* He called us to be! Hope is what keeps us moving toward the goal of living eternally in peace with God.

You not only can live in hope-filled expectancy, you can expect *change*. Yes, change. Why do you think the infomercials show you the before and after pictures of their clients? If change was not the goal, then why the effort? Jesus *expects* you to change and to live and love like Him. What was His inaugural message as He entered the public arena? "Repent, for the kingdom of heaven is near" (Matthew 3:2). Repent literally means "to change your mind," but it also implies behavioral changes based on your changed thinking. I interpret Jesus' message to be, "Change how you live because the kingdom of heaven is here." Jesus' presence and call alone are catalysts for change in our lives. To live a kingdom-of-heaven lifestyle requires I change how I am living now. His presence as the Christ, the Expected One, means we must change in order to live differently now that He is present with us. *Expect change! Embrace a new way of living.* That is precisely why Jesus came, lived, died, and rose again.

One Last Takeaway

As you work to become like Jesus, the Holy Spirit will work on your heart-relationships every day, in every way. It may be subtle at first, but eventually you'll find yourself replacing old habits with new and destructive attitudes with encouraging ones. These are changes that only God can permanently make, but they all bring with them a God-guarantee: trust Him, follow Him, and pattern your days after Him and you will soon become a changed person. It might show up as a more relaxed countenance on your once scowling face, or it might mean slipping into a smaller dress size, or it might even manifest itself as a renewed commitment to honor your body as the temple God created it to be.

It might also mean loving those hardest to love in our lives and in society. Jesus expects us to love others fully like the Father loves us, not to become religiously perfect people. We are able to live and love like Jesus because He first loved us. One of the most honorable ways of working toward being like Jesus is by practicing spiritual wellness everywhere, everyplace, and every time we encounter others.

For most of us, this means a change of lifestyle which may be slower and more off the paths upon which we currently "do life." It also means not living so much in the margin regarding the time and effort we commit to spiritual practices. And it also means ramping up our inclination to allow the Holy Spirit to change us into the likeness of Jesus—and this, my friend, is no small concession. As Christ followers, we are to live in hope-filled certainty that the summit of our lives is "peace with God" and, in that hope, we can face the struggles and suffering that may come our way as we bring the peace of God into our relationships.

Questions for Reflection

1. Why are you motivated to pursue spiritual wellness?

2. If the where of spiritual wellness is a lifestyle, what could that lifestyle look like now in your life?

3. If the when of spiritual wellness is a 24/7 life in Christ, when will you make time in your life to practice the exercises in this book so you can grow into the characteristics Jesus has revealed in the Beatitudes?

4. What changes can you anticipate by saying yes to following Jesus on the journey of spiritual wellness?

NOTES

INTRODUCTION

[1]The content of this book has been adapted from C. Gene Wilkes, *With All My Soul: God's Design for Spiritual Wellness* (Nashville: LifeWay Press, 2001). All rights reserved. Used with permission.

[2]Portions of this story were first published as "Good Excuses, Bad Results," in *Christian Health* (LifeWay), July 2001, 5.

CHAPTER 1

[1]Eugene H. Peterson, *The Contemplative Pastor* (Grand Rapids, MI: Wm. Eerdmans, 1989), 19–21.

[2]J. Oswald Chambers, *My Utmost for His Highest*, "*Missionary Munitions*," September 10.

[3]Kenneth Cooper, "Does Faith-Based Fitness Make Sense Today?" *Faith & Fitness Magazine*, April/May 2007.

[4]"Spirituality and Stress Relief: Make the Connection," www.mayoclinic.com; *italics mine.*

[5]"Plans to Prosper: A Patient Guide to Faith and Health," www.researchchannel.org/prog/displayevent (accessed July 27, 2010).

[6]Cooper, "Does Faith-Based Fitness Make Sense Today?"

CHAPTER 2

[1]Warren Wiersbe, *Five Secrets of Living* (Carol Stream, IL: Tyndale, 1978), p. 29.

[2]R. T. France, *The Gospel of Matthew, New International Commentary on the New Testament* (Grand Rapids, MI: Wm. B. Eerdmans, 2007), 114.

[3] Ibid.

[4]Allan Ross, http://bible.org/seriespage/beatitudes-matthew-51-12; accessed 4/27/2012.

[5]Dale Fletcher, "Spirituality and Health—The Real Connection is Our Relationship with God," November 8, 2011; http://www.faithandhealthconnection.org/blog/page/26/ (accessed April 27, 2012).

[6]Dallas Willard, *The Spirit of the Disciplines* (New York: Harper & Row, 1988), 68.

CHAPTER 3

[1]William Barclay, *The Gospel of Matthew* (Louisville, KY: Westminster John Knox Press. 2001), vol. 86.

[2]Richard Foster, *Celebration of Discipline* (San Francisco: HarperSanFrancisco, 1988) 96.

CHAPTER 4

[1]John Ortberg, *The Life You've Always Wanted* (Grand Rapids, MI: Zondervan, 1997), 122.

[2]Peter Scazzero, *The Emotionally Healthy Church* (Grand Rapids, MI: Zondervan, 2003), 69.

CHAPTER 5

[1]See a fuller description of the adoption idea in C. Gene Wilkes, *My Identity in Christ* (Nashville: LifeWay Press, 1999), 113.

[2]Ronald Heifetz and Marty Linsky, *Leadership on the Line: Staying Alive Through the Dangers of Leading* (Waterton, MA: Harvard Business Press, 2002), 227.

[3]John Nolland, *The Gospel of Matthew: A Commentary on the Greek Text* (Grand Rapids, MI: Wm. B. Eerdmans, 2005), 201.

[4]C. Gene Wilkes, *Jesus on Leadership*, (Carol Stream, IL: Tyndale, 1998), 23.

CHAPTER 6

[1]Charles Swindoll, "Simply Put—Applying the Beatitudes," *Insight for Living*, Australia, New Zealand, South Pacific, http://insight.asn.au/newsletters.php?item=115 (accessed February 10, 2012).

[2]J. P. Louw and E. A. Nida, *Greek-English Lexicon of the New Testament: Based on Semantec Domains*, electronic ed. of 2nd ed. (New York: United Bible Societies, 1996). 743

[3]Charles R. Swindoll, "A promise for 'those who hunger and thirst for righteousness," (September 29, 2011), *Insight for Today, Insight for Living*, http://www.insight.org/library/inight-for-today/a-promise-for-those-who-hunger.html (accessed February 10, 2012).

[4]Mark Buchanan, *The Rest of God: Restoring Your Soul by Restoring Sabbath* (Nashville: W Publishing Group, 2006), 50.

CHAPTER 7

[1]C. Gene Wilkes, *Jesus on Leadership*, student ed. (Nashville: LifeWay, 1999), 39.

[2]http://www.urbandictionary.com/thesaurus.php?term=slacktivism (accessed March 9, 2012).

[3]Dallas Willard, *The Spirit of the Disciplines* (New York: Harper&Row, 1988), 205.

CHAPTER 8

[1]http://www.trinitystudycenter.com/mount/matthew_5-7-8.php (accessed March 11, 2012).

[2]Norman Blackaby and Gene Wilkes, *Character: The Pulse of a Disciple's Heart* (Birmingham, AL: New Hope Publishers, 2012), 20.

[3]Tony Jones, *The Sacred Way: Spiritual Practices for Everyday Life* (Grand Rapids, MI: Zondervan, 2005), 164.

CHAPTER 9

[1]Philip Yancey, *Prayer: Does It Make a Difference?* (Grand Rapids, MI: Zondervan, 2006), 124.

Appendix A

With All My Soul: God's Design for Spiritual Wellness[1]
"Train yourself to be godly" (1 Timothy 4:7)

Jesus' Blessing to:	The People	The Characteristic
Poor in Spirit	Need a Savior	Spiritual poverty
Mourn	Loss of innocence and grief for wrongs	Grief that leads to repentance (2 Corinthians 7:10)
Meek	Gentle, unassertive, ready for a leader	Power under control, submission
Hunger and Thirst for God	Starving for a relationship with God	Survival appetite for the things of God; want to be right
Merciful	Heart for God and others; kind people	God's heart, a gift of the Spirit
Pure in Heart	Focused life based on uncluttered heart	Cleansed heart, God's work (Nathanael)
Peacemakers	Make peace; want to see God-change in others	Bring the peace of Christ to rule in every relationship
Persecuted	Beat up for trying to live for God	Quiet acceptance of reactions to the rule of Christ

THE PROMISE	THE ILLNESS	THE EXERCISE
The kingdom of God!	Try harder or give up	Solitude and Silence 1 Kings 19
Comfort! Isaiah 61:2	Depression Judas	Confession in Community 1 John 1:9
The earth = inheritance Romans 8:17	Codependency or overcompensate	Submission and accountability 1 Peter 5:6
Filled up	Fill hunger with ungodly things	Sabbath Rest Exodus 20
Will receive more mercy from God and others	Take on the load of others to point of destruction	Simplicity Matthew 6:33
See God and His ways; Jesus John 1:18	Hypocrisy	Fasting
Reputation for being a child of God	Keep peace; force peace; use natural ways to achieve it	Prayer
The kingdom of God!	Give up; martyr complex; push back	A complete program of spiritual disciplines

[1]Life in the valley drives us to encounter God who transforms us to return to the valley to be a peacemaker to those we live with.

SCRIPTURE INDEX

MATTHEW (continued)

MARK

LUKE

JOHN

ACTS

ROMANS

Exercise Journal

Exercise Journal